Get on your bike

Rebecca Charlton, Robert Hicks and Hannah Reynolds

Published 2014 by Bloomsbury Publishing Plc,
50 Bedford Square, London WC1B 3DP

ISBN (print) 978-1-4729-0404-1

ISBN (epub) 978-1-4729-0405-8

A CIP catalogue record for this book is available from the British Library

This book is produced using paper that is made from wood grown
in managed sustainable forests. It is natural, renewable and recyclable.
The logging and manufacturing processes conform to the environmental
regulations of the country of origin.

Design: Nicola Liddiard, Nimbus Design

Printed in China by Toppan Leefung Printing Ltd

10 9 8 7 6 5 4 3 2 1

NOTE

Whilst every effort has been made to ensure that the
content of this book is as technically accurate and
as sound as possible, neither the authors nor the
publishers can accept responsibility for any injury or
loss sustained as a result of the use of this material.

Introduction

We all know we should take more exercise, that it is good for our health, but sometimes finding the time or the motivation can be difficult. We don't believe exercising should be a chore and with cycling it isn't. Fun comes first but as an added bonus you will lose weight, have more energy and improve your health. Whether you are riding your bike to the shops, commuting to work or meeting friends for a café run, it all adds up.

Whilst our Olympic heroes and Tour de France winners provide inspiration, we want to prove that this wonderful sport is not just for the elite and can enrich many people's lives. Anyone can take to two wheels and find happiness and improve their wellbeing, armed with the right resources. Over the coming pages we explain exactly how to get on your bike, from getting started to combating nerves and finding confidence in traffic. This book will arm you with everything you need to know in order to get the most out of your cycling.

We've met ordinary riders who have coped with depression, lost weight, found love and improved their lifestyle dramatically since taking to two wheels. Whatever your sporting desires we have the tips to allow you to get the most out of your trusty bicycle. That may be riding to meet friends for a coffee or aiming to drop a couple of clothes sizes through

regular time in the saddle, or maybe you're working up to a big event.

Whether you've not yet bought a bike or want to upgrade but want to make the most of your cycling time, this book is for you.

Your journey starts here.

Rebecca Charlton

Robert Hicks

Hannah Reynolds

 Contents

Get on your
bike

Foreword

Four years ago I had no idea that I would go from being critically, even terminally ill and having to learn how to walk again, to cycling across countries and continents; and contributing to a charity fundraising effort totalling nearly £2 million.

In November 2008 doctors found an 11.5cm tumour wedged between my spine, kidney and bowel. Due to complications, in February 2009 I developed septicaemia peritonitis and was given a less than five per cent chance of survival. I dropped from 14 to six stone in weight. After being kept in a coma I had to find a way to entirely rebuild myself, including learning basic skills like walking, all over again.

A year after being diagnosed I announced I would cycle across America to raise money for the people who had helped my family and I through this time. My intention was to complete the challenge a year to the day of being given the all clear on 23 July 2010.

All was going well until day 22. Just outside of New Orleans, a truck travelling at 70mph hit me, putting me back in hospital. The ride was over.

Not being one to give up, in January 2011 I returned to the USA and started the ride again from Los Angeles, cycling 3473 miles in 24 days (with no rest days) and finishing in Miami.

In June 2011 the cancer returned but I have since been given the all-clear following more surgery, chemotherapy and radiotherapy.

In this time I've also become a father to Freddie, something I was told would never happen. I now live with Freddie and my wife, Louise.

Cycling has bought me so much and I plan to continue breaking records and boundaries. It has given me a sense of purpose, a reason to carry on. Not only that but it has taken me to some of the most beautiful places in the world, and I have met some truly wonderful people.

The bicycle has changed my life for the better, and without it, I don't know where I would be. I believed the impossible was possible and you can do anything you set your mind to. What's your excuse?

James Golding
2013

1

Benefits of the bike

Cycling changes lives. It's a bold statement but it's incredible how a humble bicycle can bring so much to its rider, way beyond the more obvious benefits of exercise.

Whether you want a flat stomach, a lifestyle overhaul or a way to find freedom we're confident you can discover happiness on two wheels.

So, first things first: you'll need to get started, find the right bike for you and decide what you want from your cycling. This sport means different things to everyone and what's right for one rider may not work for you. This book will arm you with everything you need to know to Get on your bike! but, for starters, and a bit of motivation, here's what a regular pedal has bought to the lives of these riders.

Teresa Houghton 'Cake.'

Sam Smith 'It's one of the few places I feel at peace with myself, even in the hubbub of London traffic. It's easy meditation. And fun.'

Rider Reilhan 'For me, cycling means escape.'

Greg Anderson 'Looking pro, going fast, getting better, always fun.'

Alan Laws 'I only need one word: FREEDOM.'

Michael Hillman 'Fitness, excitement, adrenaline, travel, socialising and fun!'

Gary Lake 'Everything.'

Russell Findlay 'Setting outrageous challenges and then achieving them, and it's a cool way to get around town.'

Sophie Radcliffe 'Freedom, fitness, power, fun.'

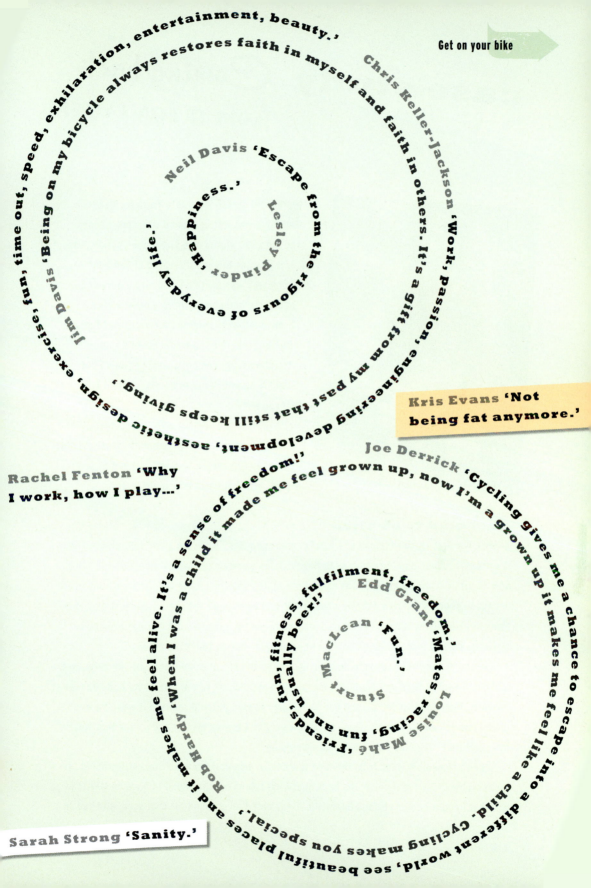

Get on your bike

Chris Keller-Jackson 'Work, passion, engineering development, aesthetic design', exercise, fun, time out, speed, exhilaration, entertainment, beauty.'

Jim Davis 'Being on my bicycle always restores faith in myself and faith in others. It's a gift from my past that still keeps giving.'

Neil Davis 'Escape from the rigours of everyday life.'

Lesley Pinder 'Happiness.'

Kris Evans 'Not being fat anymore.'

Rachel Fenton 'Why I work, how I play...'

Joe Derrick 'Cycling gives me a chance to escape into a different world, see beautiful places and it makes you special.'

Rob Hardy 'When I was a child it made me feel grown up, now I'm a grown up it makes me feel like a child. Cycling makes you feel alive. It's a sense of freedom!'

Edd Grant 'Mates, racing, fun, fitness, fulfilment, freedom.'

Louise Mahé 'Friends, Make, fun and usually beer!'

Stuart MacLean 'Fun.'

Sarah Strong 'Sanity.'

Coming back from a car crash

Essex-based triathlete **Jackie** Stretton, 26, was left in a coma when she became the innocent victim of a high-speed police chase.

Hit by car thieves travelling at 100mph her hatchback was sent head-on into a pursuing police car and she suffered a broken back, broken leg and sustained a serious head injury. Doctors told her she would never be able to take part in competitive sport again but Jackie wasn't ready to give up. Here's her inspirational story.

'Before the crash, I was always an adventure racer. I enjoyed multi-sport events, ideally the longer, the better. I had hoped to become a sponsored athlete in 2012.

Just glad to be alive

'I think the first thing I remember when I came round was, 'wow, I'm alive' followed by 'ooh, it's breakfast time and they have bran flakes'. I don't remember panicking about not being able to move. I think whatever was said to me while I was unconscious must have sunk in because I seemed to know exactly where I was and what had happened. I was just glad that I was awake and my family was there. I wanted to get up and walk and was determined I would be able to, even though I only just had enough energy to lift my arms.

'On one of the first days after waking up, I tried to get out of bed while the nurse wasn't looking. I wanted to have a wander. I managed to pull myself to the side of my bed and lean forward. Then I almost fell off the bed and nearly passed out and realised it wasn't a good idea. I had to call for help to lie me back down again. I scared myself and I think that was the point that I realised how hard things would be.

'I don't remember a lot from the first few days in hospital because I was still coming off the morphine. But I remember the back specialist telling me that I had to have an MRI scan and that I might need a serious operation. I was petrified going in for that scan, and had to wait 24 hours for the result. When I got the good news that the fracture was stable and all the nerves and spinal cord were OK, I sobbed my heart out. I felt like the luckiest girl in the world!

'There were so many hard parts to deal with. When I got home from hospital, I needed 24-hour care. I couldn't brush my own teeth, had to have bed baths and couldn't lift myself up to sit or stand up to go to the toilet. I needed help with everything. I had never felt so helpless before.

'The very worst part was the day my leg cast came off. I had lost a lot of weight anyhow, but my leg was nothing but skin and bone; there was no muscle whatsoever. It was scary. I couldn't bend my leg even a few degrees, no matter how hard I tried and I honestly thought I would never walk again. I couldn't see the light at the end of the tunnel and it was so hard to imagine that I'd ever been able to use that leg to win races in the past.

Getting started again

'I started having physio sessions, and trying various exercises to get the flexibility back, but it was such a long, slow process. Even now, my right leg still can't bend to the same degree as my left leg, and I doubt it ever will again, despite my hardest efforts.

'I also had bleeding on the brain, so was in an induced coma for three days. My family had been warned that I might not recognise them when I woke up. I had broken my right kneecap and my back so I was in a back brace for four months instead. It was very restrictive, painful and uncomfortable, but a I felt it was a much better option than surgery to insert bolts.

'I've got a few scars now, but to me, they symbolise strength and determination. When the doctor told me I might never race again, I was a little bit naive about it. I decided that he didn't know me, and hadn't seen me race, so couldn't decide whether I would still be able to or not. How could he know something like that?

'I took every obstacle on in small stages. Once I got home, I focused on trying to stand up by myself. Once I did that, I would try and walk for five minutes. Then the next day, I would try to get my own food. I broke everything down into manageable chunks to try and achieve the every day tasks.

A target to aim at

'It was when I was looking online that I saw an Ironman event called City to Summit in Scotland and broke down. I figured I would never be able to do that event because the doctors had told me I would never race again. And then I got angry. Why shouldn't I be able to do it? Why should two silly boys in a stolen car change my life forever? So I booked it!

'Having an aim was invaluable. It meant that every day I woke up, I had something to focus on, and every small achievement was one step closer to the finish line. That finish line was all the strength I needed. I became very determined. I didn't want anyone else deciding my fate for me, so I chose to push myself and prove them wrong: when you dream big, anything is possible.

'My only focus was the Ironman. The doctors had told me if there was anything I wouldn't be able to do, it was trail running. I had lost my posterior cruciate ligament when I broke my knee, and had been told that I would possibly need surgery to make my leg stable. However, if I were to build the strength in my quadriceps, they would do the job.

Cycling and my recovery

'The doctors told me cycling was my answer. I had only ever owned a mountain bike and had always been a little nervous about trying a road bike because I was under the impression they were a lot harder to control and I would probably have a bad accident. The car crash made me realise that you can have an accident in the simplest of situations, so I may as well do what I considered to be risky. So I bought my first road bike. I wasn't able to ride it for about two months because I couldn't get on it with my injuries, but I could look at it for motivation. That was the bike that would get me across Scotland. As cycling is non-impact, the physios were happy with me pedalling away to my heart's content. They would tell me off for running.

'Spinning in the gym was a safe environment for me. I felt comfortable because I knew I was surrounded by others should something go wrong, but I also felt independent because I was making my body whole again. It wasn't injuring me further – it was fixing me.

'My first outing on my road bike was both petrifying and exhilarating. I was only out for a few miles, but I felt like I was on top of the world. I had conquered my injuries and my fears.

'I had followed Movistar's Alex Dowsett as a cyclist for years because he was the guy from just up the road who had inspired me to cycle in the first place. He used the same training grounds as I did, had overcome serious injury too, and look at what he had achieved!

'At the start of each month I took pictures of my legs so that I could see the difference that the cycling was making, and I still look back at those pictures now in amazement. The change was incredible. From not having the ability to bend my knee, to managing to get from one side of Scotland to other using nothing but the power in my injured legs is such an incredible achievement. I had done it. I had fought the odds and proved everyone wrong. And that was the start of my new life.'

The list of cycling benefits continues from helping in overcoming serious injury to managing illness. Business manager **Jeremy Hayden**, 44, was diagnosed with Type 2 diabetes in 2009 and it was a wake-up call. He has used cycling to improve his health significantly and now he tells us why he's better off by bike.

'Bikes have always been with me: as a kid, through my teenage years, the first mountain bikes and then the road.

'I was a big lad though, so I chose other sports. I was built for rugby, and I was not a climber. And so that was as far as it went. I still rode, but never with any real intent.

'Then, after too many years of neglect and high living, I found out I was a type 2 diabetic, and was told by the doctor and diabetic nurse that I needed to make some changes. And soon.

'The first thing I tackled was obviously my diet. As I watched my food intake, little by little the kilos started to come off.

'I can tell you that this feels good. So as the springtime approached I got back onto my bikes, gradually building the miles up. I was feeling good: stronger, fitter, lighter, and just loving that I was improving.

'And I've just kept on doing it. Twenty-five kilos have gone; the bike has provided a means, a measure and a reward.

'It's not been without its setbacks: trying to sit on with the fast lads on a hilly Sunday morning 100k was a wake up call. So you step back, take some advice, do the training and try again in three months time.

'Not every ride can be your best ever, but when you have a good one, there's not much to beat it.

'Cycling is whatever you want it to be. You can always be better, if that's what you want. Or if you're happy to just head out for a bimble along the cycle track on a sunny Sunday, that's good too.

'Get out there and do it. And keep doing it, only good can come of it.'

case study *Beating the black dog*

It's well documented that exercise can have a significant impact on your mood but for **Stevie Wood**, 37, cycling meant the difference between suffering with depression and seeing a path through it all.

'Cycling, along with my family, means the world to me. Cycling is in my blood. It's a way forward rather than a thing to dwell on: something to be excited about constantly, permanently and a way of being productive.

'Cycling is the difference between a positive and negative me. On a daily basis I am more than aware of whether it's a ride day, a training day or a dreaded rest day. These three can be the difference between positive and happy, positive and motivated or on the rest day heading towards the unhappy side of life.

'Cycling is a massive factor in my mood as it gives me focus. I fill my year with various events, tests, races and challenges that are all within the boundaries of 'being allowed' in a family environment.

'My entire year has a focus or many focuses. Next year I will be taking part in a seven day attempt at the Lands End to John O'Groats (LEJOG) cycle ride, taking part in British Cycling racing for the first time at 37 years of age and also having a second attempt at a 24-hour time trial among many other events and challenges.

'All of this helps with depression and has turned my outlook round a full 180 degrees. I have focus, aims, goals and a seriously healthy lifestyle. I give myself little or no time to become depressed, as my life is so full. Everything I do is with the full consent, help and guidance of my family and that is the big part of beating depression to me. My outlook on life and cycling especially has been transmitted to the rest of my family and friends. My wife now regularly cycles, my son has begun racing and my daughter also cycles. At no point have I told or forced anyone to take part in cycling they have seen the effects first hand with me and want a piece of it, they also want to spend more time with me as a result.

'So if you're feeling bad, sad or down, just get out on a bike: towpath, mountain, road or bridleway, it doesn't matter! They all have the same effect: relief! It doesn't matter how far or where you go, the freedom you can find on a bike opens your whole life to a new kind of inner freedom. After your first ride you will be hooked, this will give you focus, aims and goals as it has done for me. You'll have little time to sit and listen to the demons within.'

Where to start

2

What type of cycling?

If you haven't already got a bike, or the rusting heap in the back of the garage isn't up to the job, then the first thing you are going to need to get started on your cycling journey is a bike! There is a huge range of types of bike available so before you even set foot in a bike shop it is worth asking yourself a few questions about what kind of cycling you want to do. Below we look at the different genre of bicycle available and what kind of riding they are most suited to.

Road bike

Road bikes are designed purely for tarmac. They are sleek and fast with drop handle bars for a racy aerodynamic position and skinny tyres for minimal rolling resistance. However, even within this group of bikes there are many varieties. Sportive bikes have been designed to offer a slightly more relaxed position for those not wanting the super-hunched style of a Tour de France racer but want to be as fast and efficient as possible.

Fixed gear bikes and single-speeds also come under the category of road bikes. Fixies have become incredibly popular in the last few years, whereas before it was purely cycle couriers using them they are now the favoured style of hipsters everywhere. A single-speed is slightly easier to handle, as unlike a fixed gear where the pedals turn with the wheels, a free wheel allows you to stop pedalling which can be easier in traffic.

Mountain bike

A mountain bike is most at home on rugged trails. With suspension forks at the front and often suspension at the rear too they are designed to soak up rocks, ruts and drops allowing you to ride anywhere, no matter how challenging the terrain. Big fat tyres also add to the comfort but, most importantly, provide grip on difficult surfaces such as mud as the knobbles dig into the surface for traction and drive. A more upright riding position and wide bars give the rider room to move around the bike and adjust their position to handle the challenges of the ground they are riding over.

A pure mountain bike is slow to ride on tarmac as the thick, heavy tyres create a lot of drag and the suspension system wastes energy on smooth surfaces. Often mountain bikes are considerably heavier than road bikes so while geared lower for easier climbing off-road the weight makes them slow and cumbersome on tarmac ascents. Buy a mountain bike if you fancy the adrenalin rush and challenge of learning new off-road techniques and you want your bike to take you deep into the countryside and way off the beaten track.

Hybrids

Hybrids blend together the assets of both mountain bikes and road bikes. The position is more upright, affording you a good view of where you are going, easing the pressure on your lower back and allowing you to comfortably move around on the bike. Wide flat bars mean that handling is stable and predictable making them a good choice for riding in traffic. Hybrids have only front suspension or no suspension at all.

However not all hybrids are equal, some lean more toward the mountain bike style and others more toward the road. You can buy a hybrid with the same big wheels and skinny tyres as a road bike which will be nippy and fast on tarmac or opt for a hybrid with fatter tyres that will still allow you to venture off-road on easier terrain such as tow-paths, park land and gravel tracks.

Town bike

Dutch style town bikes or utility bikes are stylish and practical. They are easy to ride, stable in their handling and offer a comfortable upright position with good view of the road ahead. Bikes can come fitted with baskets or panniers making them great for doing your shopping or transporting goods. They are often quite heavy but have nice easy gears so can cope with most gradient changes. Their style encourages relaxed riding and they are the ultimate choice for short visits into town and journeys of only a few miles at a time.

Folding bike

Whilst Brompton has become synonymous with folding bikes there are many other brands to choose from. A folding bike is a practical choice for commuters and flat dwellers with limited storage space. Bikes are not allowed in or out of London stations at rush hour so folding bikes handily get round this problem by tucking between seats or fitting on the luggage rack. Emerge from Waterloo station and you'd be forgiven for thinking it was the folding bike World Championships as hundreds of commuters mass at the lights waiting for the green 'Go' signal.

A folding bike is perfect for commuting over short distances but its small wheels and compromised position means it is not the ideal choice for longer rides or challenging hilly terrain; however there are numerous people who have set out to prove otherwise and folding bikes have been ridden from John O'Groats to Land's End and around the circumference of the British Isles. If a folding bike is all you have room for it doesn't exclude you from any kind of road riding.

Cyclo-cross bike

Cyclo-cross began as a form of winter racing: events were fast and furious lasting only an hour. In recent years cyclo-cross bikes have broken out of the racing niche and are now used by many cyclists as versatile commuting bikes and for longer leisure rides and even off-road sportive events. They resemble road bikes with drop handlebars but

have wider, knobbly tyres, greater clearance for mud and lower gears so that they can be ridden off-road.

A cross bike makes a great commuting bike as its riding position is slightly more relaxed than that of a pure road bike. Many cross-bikes are now designed so that you can fit mudguards and panniers if you fancy a go at touring but equally if you fit a good set of tyres you could tear up your local woods or take on a long distance off-road challenge such as the South Downs Way.

Touring bikes

Touring bikes are the workhorses of the cycling world; they are designed to carry loads and come fitted with mudguards and a pannier rack. Load your bike up with everything you need and you have the ultimate in cycling freedom; you can go for a day, a week, a month or a year. It could be a trip to the shops or a circumnavigation of the globe. Bikes need to be robust because of the weight they will carry and because it is distance travelled, not speed that makes the touring cyclist tick.

The riding position is designed with comfort in mind as the pace will be slow and the hours in the saddle long. A longer than usual wheelbase makes a touring bike stable when

loaded with gear and the handling easy and predictable. Gears are low to accommodate the extra weight that you will be carrying. Touring bikes are generally made from more flexible materials than race bikes such as steel or titanium; weight isn't as important and the less rigid materials smooth out the bumps in the road.

Me and my bike

I love my road bike because...

'Road riding gives you a great sense of freedom and I love my Speccy Tarmac SL pro. It's fast, responsive and never lets me down. My job involves me sitting down for 90 per cent of the day so riding my bike to and from work and at weekends gives me the freedom to clear my head and keep fit.

'Riding a bicycle is a skill that you can learn. It's like communicating and learning. If you're willing to work at it, you can rapidly improve the quality of every part of your life.'

Mat Pennell

I love my hybrid because...

Everything about my hybrid I love. The fact that I can whizz around the roads of where I live at a fast and furious pace and then a moment later, take it easy for a gentle spin – it doesn't look out of place if you do either.

'I've always suffered from a bad back, and the position on the hybrid is much more 'back friendly' than some other road bikes. I've never really been a fan of dropped handlebars – I don't see myself as a racer – so the wide handlebars are perfect for me. I've also found that as I'm more upright, I'm much more observant of what is happening around me.'

Chris Hicks

Shannon Durrant

I love my single speed because...

'Cycling isn't just about getting from A to B. It's sometimes about, getting from A to B and feeling like you've pushed hard to earn that trendy Hoxton facial hair. With just one gear you have cycling in its purest form. You get out the saddle, swing the bars from side to side, feel that cro-mo frame flex with each downward pedal stroke and hear your tyres snaking as they grip the asphalt. There is no leaver to change gear. You just breathe in, dig deep and crank it up that hill.'

I love my folding bike because...

'The bicycle was the best invention of all time ... until Brompton went and put a hinge in the middle of it, making the best portable and now even better. My folder is brilliant because normal bikes are banned from most trains, tubes and buses. With the Brompton I'm free to combine pedal power with public transport, taking the train over long distances and cycling through the congested parts where a bike is still the fastest form of transport in the world. You'd love it too — imagine never having to pay for a taxi again, or top up your Oyster card.'

Jamie Darlow

I love my cyclo-cross bike because...

'Cyclo-cross is probably the most accessible of all competitive bike races. It's friendly and fun and – as you're often riding on grass or in sloppy mud it is fairly low risk. But if you are competitive and you're racing properly it can be very tough.

You can't really be dropped from a cross race so you are always in the mix even if you are riding around on your own. You engage in little battles with riders around you, races within the race, so you push all the way to the chequered flag.

There is a specific set of skills that help you in cyclo-cross. You can get by without many of them but once you have mastered one it feels great and really improves your racing. You are constantly learning for your first two or three seasons, probably more.

'You can get a competitive cyclo-cross bike for a comparatively small outlay and then you have the most versatile bike you can own. Cross bikes are designed to be tough, comfortable and fast so beyond the race they are great winter trainers, commuters and many of them can even be set up for touring.

Cyclo-cross has improved my fitness and bike-handling skills and I've made some good friends through racing. I've raced in bone-dry dust, through hub-deep puddles and even in heavy snow, so it's a great way to stay riding all year round.'

Matt Levett

I love my touring bike because...

'Riding my touring bike gives me the ultimate sense of freedom: paring down your belongings to an amount you can carry makes you realise how little you actually need to get by, and it makes life very simple. With everything in your panniers you are completely self-sufficient; you can go for a night, a week, or a month. I sometimes fantasise about what it would be like to just keep pedalling and see where I end up and with a touring bike you can. Once you set off on

your adventure there is no limit to where you can go or how long for. With a tent you can stop and make your bed for the night where ever you fancy, give yourself time to stop and explore, stay as long as you like and when you have had enough pack up and move on. A holiday on a touring bike can be both the ultimate in adventure and the perfect antidote to the little niggles and stresses of every day life.'

Hannah Reynolds

I love my mountain bike because...

'As much as I love my road bike as a tool to get fit and ride to work on, my mountain bike is my first love. I love nothing more than heading out into the hills of a weekend for a great ride with a group of like-minded mates. The thrill of the descents is matched by the banter and the camaraderie. And the scenery once you get away from the roads and the towns can't be beaten. My mountain bike has taken me to some amazing locations around the country and the world and has supplied me with some of the best mates, and times, of my life.'

Ben Smith

How to buy a bike

Your local bike shop is the obvious place to start, not just because you can actually go in and touch and try the bikes you are interested in, but because it is worth making friends with your bike shop right at the beginning of your adventure into cycling. Bike shops are generally staffed by knowledgeable and passionate bike riders who like nothing more than the opportunity to share their knowledge. Don't be afraid to ask questions because they can be a great source of tips and advice.

Buying a bike from a shop as opposed to an on-line retailer means that you get a much better service and even if the bike costs fractionally more you'll benefit from all kinds of extras. All shops will provide the bike safety checked and ready to ride, most will offer a service after a certain period of time to check that everything on the bike has bedded in correctly and to check it is still running sweetly. If, when you choose your bike there are

Other places to look

EBay • Great for bargains but you need to know what you are looking for and have a good idea of its value. Also beware that many stolen bikes end up being sold through E-bay. Ask if the seller has any documentation and look to see if it has been post-coded or has any other way of checking the ownership.

Online retailers • Again great for bargains but you are unable to try the bike for size or give it a test ride. Sneaky people will go to a bike shop, do the test ride, and then buy on-line. We say support your local retailer because they can do much more than just sell you a bike.

Police auctions • If the police recover a bike and it is not claimed within a certain time frame they will auction it off. You can get some tremendous bargains and although you may feel uncomfortable buying a bike you know has been stolen you can be assured the police will have done everything possible to locate the owner first. Ask at your local police station for details of nearby auctions. Find out more at *www.police-information.co.uk*

items that you aren't sure of: maybe you fancy a different saddle or would like better pedals, a shop will be able to negotiate some kit swaps and make the changes for you.

As your cycling develops you will discover you need new items: an upgrade for your bike, a better pair of shoes. By building a relationship with your shop they'll get to know your riding style and tastes and be able to recommend the best products for you. You might also find you strike up friendships with other customers and many shops now offer evening or weekend rides from the shop led by a member of staff.

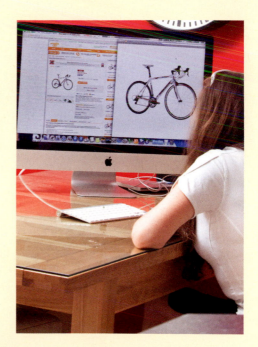

3

Gear, the basics

Getting kitted out with the right gear will make the world of difference to your cycling pursuits. A comfortable ride makes for a far more enjoyable experience but with so many options available it can be hard to choose exactly what you need to get started, or to take your riding to the next level.

First, the vast choices on the market mean you don't have to re-mortgage the house to purchase the basics but equally, the sky's the limit if you have some cash burning a hole in your pocket.

What's more, you don't have to conform to a certain cyclists' uniform. The choice is yours and whatever your style, we've got plenty of tips to get you fitted up.

The long and short of it

First things first, cycling-specific shorts are an absolute must. They contain a pad in the saddle area, often referred to as a chamois, and if you only ever buy one piece of kit, this should be it.

Riding with a good pair of cycling shorts means you can pedal for longer and they should help you to avoid bruising, chafing or soreness in your nether regions. It's not the most pleasant dinner table chat but looking after your chamois zone should be a priority, especially if you're hopping on the bike on a daily basis. Adding antibacterial cream will further prevent against saddle sore nasties.

The next question usually asked is, 'do I wear pants with my cycling kit?' and the answer is an unequivocal 'no'! Cycling shorts are designed to be worn against your skin and not only will boxers or knickers nullify the technical benefits but the seams and non-breathable material will make things rather uncomfortable. It may seem like an alien concept at first but you will quickly get used to it.

If you're brand new to cycling or starting on a new riding position, such as switching from a hybrid to a road bike, it's perfectly normal to experience a bit of bruising in your seat bone area. After your first long ride you may find it a bit painful getting back on for a second time, but this will quickly subside and if it doesn't, you may want to consider changing your saddle to something a bit more comfy as everyone's personal preference is different.

A clean pair of shorts with a good pad should keep you pain-free but should you experience saddle discomfort, take a couple of days off the bike to recover and smother on some anti-bacterial cream.

The next question is usually 'bibs or no bibs?' Bib shorts may look reminiscent of the circus but they keep things in place nicely when you're riding, increasing comfort and effective fit. When it comes to going to the toilet many women like to go for a waistband rather than a bib but there are plenty of innovative solutions available to help you whip them off more quickly when nature calls!

Kitting up

In the summertime, clothing options are pretty straightforward. A cycling top and shorts will usually suffice on dry days if you want to go for the Lycra look. Or for a more modest

look, cycling shorts can be hidden beneath baggy shorts or even a skirt, or dress. As with ditching the pants, embracing super-tight spandex-esque outfits can seem a little daunting but bike-specific clothing is fit for purpose and is a great option for keeping your body temperature regulated so you don't end up dripping with sweat in ordinary clothes. That said, baggier options can be just as technical so don't let the Lycra put you off!

Arm and leg warmers (left)

To keep riding all year round you'll need to build up your basic cycling wardrobe in order to be equipped for all four seasons. Arm and leg warmers do exactly what they say on the tin and will extend a basic jersey and shorts when the weather is nippier. They'll be a godsend in autumn and spring and start at a reasonable price point. Thickness of material and quality of grippers will affect the cost.

Gloves

Not only for warmth but also for protecting your hands are a range of gloves for all seasons. Fingerless mitts are great in the summer with more heavy-duty thick materials being necessary throughout the winter months. For extreme cold weather silk liners can bolster thick gloves.

Rain jackets

When it comes to wet weather jackets there are a number of subcategories including shower-proof shells, wind shells and fully water proof jackets. Having a lightweight shell in your pocket to get you home in the event of an unexpected rain shower, or to protect you from a cold wind is a great fail safe. If you're planning to ride on a wet day you may want to look into more technical rainproof jackets, which won't pack as small but will save the day.

Winter layers

For the depths of winter, arm and leg warmers just won't be up to the job. If you're out for prolonged periods in the cold you'll need to shop around for long winter tights or trousers and thermal long-sleeve upper layers.

Helmets

With great looking, lightweight helmets available at bargain prices there's really no excuse not to protect your head. Ensure your choice meets EU safety standards and offers a good fit.

Baggies and casuals

Starting cycling doesn't have to mean Lycra. Baggy shorts and trousers are available to buy with a pad insert to protect you during your saddle time. Casual tops can offer plenty of wicking properties without being super-tight.

Your second skin

If you want to ride in greater comfort, then good quality base layer garments should be at the top of your most wanted list.

The reason why there is so much fuss made over base layers is because they are in direct contact with your body – think of them as a second skin which helps regulate your body temperature.

The importance of a base layer

A good base layer will be able to keep you cool in the heat of the summer while also being able to keep you warm during the coldness of winter.

What to look for

When buying a good base layer there are a few things to keep an eye out for.

• First, it must fit. It sounds like a bit of a no brainer, but you'll be amazed at how many people get this wrong.

• Wearing something too big will not keep you sufficiently insulated and sweat will not be able to leave your body.

• If it's too tight, your body won't be able to breathe, causing you to sweat excessively and saturate your garment.

• It's really important that you buy a cycling specific base layer. Again, another obvious point, but many will buy a general base layer, and while it can still be a good quality one, it won't be of much use.

• The cycling position is unique, and when you are crouching over the handlebars, you want the garment to stay close to your skin. An ordinary base layer that you may use for jogging will ride up on your lower back and start to fold at the front.

Synthetics

They can transfer moisture very quickly away from the body, but are slow to absorb it. Body odour does build up – and quickly. They can be a little tricky to keep clean.

This is due to the garment's ability to keep your body insulated while wicking away moisture from the surface of the body, keeping your body at a stable temperature.

But what's the fuss about body temperature? Well, it's very important to maintain correct body temperature especially if you're out the bike for a few hours. If your body becomes too hot, and the heat isn't able to escape your body, you will over-heat and you could become dehydrated, which could lead to exhaustion or fatigue.

On the other hand, if you aren't adequately insulated, and you aren't able to hold on to your own body warmth, you could get extremely cold very quickly.

Not only is this terribly uncomfortable, it can be rather dangerous. While getting chilled or wet is not a cause of colds, these factors can increase the chances of catching a bug.

Your body will also start shivering in a bid to stay warm. In order to do this, the body has to burn more calories than it normally would, resulting in you losing valuable energy resources. Once you get cold, it can be extremely tough to get warm again.

When you're out riding your bike, there are enough things to keep a watch out for. You don't want to be worrying about the clothes you are wearing, so invest in a good base layer for peace of mind.

Wool

Merino wool is very comfortable on the skin and offers effective moisture transportation, while keeping the skin dry. Merino doesn't pong much either.

Cotton

Great value for money although it's not one of the most effective at wicking. It will absorb moisture quickly, but is very slow to dry out.

Cycling style

Look around the streets at the many cyclists taking to the roads of Britain and it's quickly apparent that there are a number of distinct tribes. You can mix and match your style but here's a guide to just some of the various fashions, clans, cliques and respective rulebooks.

The closet cyclist

A style for the cyclist who doesn't want to admit that they're a die-hard cyclist. You don't look out of place in a coffee shop and you can leave your bike outside the pub safe in the knowledge people won't know it belongs to you. Features such as hidden padded short inserts, sweat wicking t-shirts and vests are your friend and will keep your habit a secret from onlookers. If you're not ready to embrace Lycra this is the perfect solution for you and people will treat you as a regular pub-goer and will wonder how you're burning off the beer with such ease. You'll be the envy of all your friends.

The vest: *Giselle's top comprises sweat-wicking material and secret bra support. Perfect for both towpaths and cafés alike.*

The skort: *A skirt hides the fact that closet cyclist Giselle is in fact wearing padded cycling shorts that conveniently attach underneath. Cycling brand Pearl Izumi makes this handy garment and there are plenty of similar options on the market to add a subtle performance factor to your outfit.*

Trainers: *Flat pedals accommodate whatever footwear you like but if you want to progress to clip-in pedals, trainers with recessed cleats offer a convenient solution. These will allow you to walk around without damaging the fixture or falling over, while retaining your closet cyclist status.*

The commuter

Cycling commuters come in all shapes and sizes and the rulebook is relaxed meaning anything goes. Bikes you'll see in rush hour include fixies, hybrids, mountain bikes and racy road bikes. This can be combined with baggies, Lycra, and numerous accessories.

The rucksack: *Harry is carries everything he needs to transform into work mode.*

The helmet: *Harry wears a high-viz helmet to be safe and seen in traffic. This one has a light on the front: crucial in dim light and rush hour.*

The outfit: *Baggies hide Lycra shorts underneath. The casual cycling jersey will draw the sweat away from his skin, keeping him dry where he needs it.*

The café cyclist

A café cyclist likes to mix up their style, sometimes featuring a touch of retro mixed with modern technology. Lois is wearing a classic jersey from Rapha, a British brand that you'll spot in any reputable cyclists' café. It costs a fair whack but will allow you entry into an exclusive club. You are likely to get some miles under your belt in both town and countryside but you'll look great at any café stop and you take your style seriously. You can ride though and you'll think nothing of a sprint surge from the traffic lights, but you always keep things fun. You search out unique woollen jerseys and quirky accessories. You may even go for a neck scarf at times.

The outfit: *Three quarter length tights are a compromise between casual trousers and Lycra bibshorts and the cotton jersey combines old school looks with a full zip and high performance.*

The cap: *Lois wears a cap set at a slight angle with the peak flipped up like Tour de France heroes of the past.*

The club cyclist

The typical club cyclist belongs to a pack of riders who wear matching Lycra outfits or plain kit. Cleated shoes, race-style helmets and tighter-than-tight garments are the order of the day – and it's important to wear the latest gear.

The club cyclist often dreams of being a professional rider and puts in a number of hours training on the bike. Co-ordination is the ultimate aim when it comes to this tribe's wardrobe and replica kit, such as the same riding eyewear or team edition shoes, is a must if you want to feel like a pro.

The helmet: *The club rider loves a well-ventilated helmet, while it may offer optimum air flow to your head it's most like the pro's wear and, for the club cyclist, that's a good enough reason to wear it.*

The shoes: *Your shoes will clip in to your pedals, most likely with roadie style cleats rather than the MTB style spds. These allow you maximum power transfer to pedal away from your rivals.*

The professional rider

This is the real deal, the look all club cyclists aspire to: the professional, sponsored rider. Fans scream their name over the barriers and they ride races like the Tour de France. If you want to replicate the pros you'll need to obey some rules. Never mix team kits, or do it at your peril. You won't often see a football fan in and Chelsea shirt and West Ham shorts. Pick your team and remain loyal for the season. Clashing strips don't usually work either, so pick your team colours.

We've borrowed Movistar's Alex Dowsett to demonstrate how as a pro he wears his team kit with style.

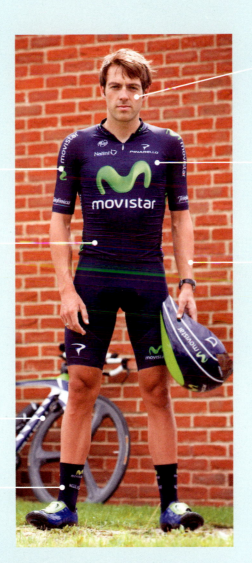

Jersey and shorts: *Branded with sponsorship to which the rider is loyal to, complete with matching team edition helmet, shoes and accessories.*

Body fat: *Extremely low, as low as 4 per cent!*

Bike: *As light as the sport's rule book allows.*

Sock length: *High, very high*

Race face: *To scare the opposition.*

Lycra: *The tighter the better.*

Tan: *It's imperative to align your shorts to the same line each time you go out to ensure crisp tan lines. To make yourself look like you've been training harder than you have, wear your shorts to a spray tan salon.*

45

4

How to get set up

How you sit on your bike and how your bike fits you will determine both your comfort and also how easy you find your bike to ride and to control. There are several different levels of bike fitting and a lot depends on the kind of bike you are riding and what kind of cycling you want to do.

Whatever bike you are buying whether it is a folder or a top end carbon racing bike it needs to fit you. Your bike shop should be able to advise with some very simple tests and recommendations, if possible ask for a test ride because how a bike 'feels' is important as well. If you are choosing a hybrid, folder or mountain bike then paying for an extensive bike fit is less crucial unless you have an injury – see box – however if you are buying a brand new road bike then having a bike fit is a great option as it can eliminate the guesswork in

Bike fit for injury

As the old rhyme reminds us, 'the head-bones connected to the...' Everything in the body is part of a kinetic chain. Clip a shoe into a pedal and the bike becomes part of the chain too. With the highly repetitive nature of pedalling a bicycle, injuries and niggles arising from poor set-up are common.

Whether it is the shoe/cleat set-up, saddle height or handlebar position, the effects on the body, through its kinetic chain from the soles of your feet right up to your neck and head, can be dramatic. If you are experiencing back or neck pain, aching shoulder, sore wrists, niggles in your knees or any other discomfort that you think may be bike related it is worth getting your position checked out by an expert.

Trained bike fitters will be able to identify problems and offer potential remedies. This could take the form of physical adjustments to bike dimensions, additional 'fitting aids' such as insoles or wedges in shoes, or in conjunction with a physiotherapist exercise and training advice to strengthen and improve areas of weakness.

choosing the right size and geometry to suit your body and riding style. It offers peace of mind that you'll be riding away on the right bike that is set-up ready for you to enjoy the experience. This service may be free as part of the sales incentive, but bear in mind some may charge an additional fee. Most retailers will be prepared to swap parts such as stems, bars, and saddles as part of the package, to improve or customise fit, and perhaps make recommendations for pedals.

Technical bike fits

If you're uncomfortable riding is no fun. This lies at the heart of any good fit, enjoying the simple pleasure of riding means not feeling like you've been beaten up every time you get off your bike. Cycling should not hurt! If it does something needs investigating. A trained bike fit technician should be able to help you find the best position for comfort and also to perform to your best on the bike. Unless you are racing comfort is the number one priority, as that will allow you to get most pleasure out of the hours you spend on your bike.

The basic way to correct saddle height

The bare minimum of bike fit is to get the saddle height right and the reach to the bars correct so that you can steer and brake safely. On any bike from a folder to a racing machine it is important to get these two things spot on. The simplest way to find your saddle height is to sit squarely in the saddle and adjust the seat height until your leg is completely straight when your heel is on the pedal. This means that when the pedal is in the correct position under the ball of your foot there will be the right degree of bend in your knee.

Gentle curve to upper back and spine so there is a clear view of the road without having to tilt the head back.

Chest slightly lifted.

Elbows slightly bent.

Hands should be roughly shoulder width apart. Wrists should not be excessively flexed.

Hip angle should not be too acute.

Saddle should be level or very slightly nose down.

Slight bend in knee

Pedal should be under the ball of the foot.

However if you want to go the full hog because you have had an injury or because you want to progress your cycling to a higher level then technology will come to your aid with cutting-edge techniques such as digital video analysis, laser sights, and sophisticated 3D motion capture software for dynamic fitting. This will give you the most comprehensive all over body and bike MOT possible.

Saddles

One of the key discomforts cyclists complain about comes from the saddle department. There are several things you can do to ensure you are sitting comfortably. First, buy yourself some decent cycling shorts with a padded insert (and remember no knickers!). Second, set your saddle up so it is level, parallel with the ground. Very slightly nose down may help ease pressure on soft tissues but nose up is a definite no-no. The way you sit on your bike can also affect how comfortable you find the saddle. If you are rolling too far forward at the pelvis you will effectively be squashing your soft tissues and it may indicate the reach of your bike is too long. Unfortunately finding the right saddle is very much down to trial and error so check all the above points first before making a new purchase. Steer away from saddles that are very wide or heavily padded. They may look incredibly comfy but the bulk can actually create additional pressure points.

How to choose shoes

Your pedals are how you connect with your bike and supply the power from your legs for your forward momentum so it's worth giving a bit of thought to the various types available. Often when you buy a bike the pedals that come on it are cheap, simple plastic ones as bike manufacturers expect you to change them to your own preferred style. We recommend that this is one of the first changes or upgrades you make to your bike.

Plastic pedals are often small and provide little grip so your feet can easily slip off the pedals, particularly on a damp day. Toe clips attach your feet securely to the pedals but they can be difficult to get out of and if the pedal is upside down will drag on the ground. While toe clips are often recommended for beginners we'd actually suggest either going for a plain flat pedal or heading straight to the type of pedal that allows you to clip your feet into them.

Clipless pedals do away for the need for toe clips, a cleat on the bottom of your shoe clips directly into the pedal securing your foot in a similar way to a ski boot to a ski binding.

To clip in you push forward and down, to clip out you gently twist your heel outward. The benefits of this system are multiple; because your foot is securely attached you are able to engage more of your leg muscles to powering the pedals as you can pull up as well as push down, being attached to the pedals helps you to feel more 'at one' with your bike and can help with your stability and balance.

Many new riders' number one fear when starting to use clipless pedals is that they won't be able to clip out fast enough in an emergency, or will simply forget to do so and topple over sideways. Every cyclist has at least one embarrassing story of falling off at traffic lights or outside a café; it's not a big deal and you rarely hurt yourself. In a crash situation the pedals release really easily so there is no risk of injury. When you are starting out, the best kind of clipless pedal is one that is flat on one side and a clip-in on the other. This means you can use ordinary shoes or cycling shoes depending on the length of your journey and in situations where you might be nervous of being clipped in you can use the flat side.

Choose your shoes

Cycling shoes are different from ordinary shoes regardless of whether you go for clipless pedals or flat pedals; the soles need to be stiff so that they don't flex when you press down on the pedals. While you can of course pedal a bike in any type of shoe, a soft-soled shoe such as a running shoe will result in a lot of wasted energy. The other important thing to consider with your shoe choice is the lace. If a shoelace comes undone it can easily get wrapped around the crank or caught in your chain and could cause an accident. Look for shoes with a wrap over Velcro strap to secure the laces or ones with no laces at all.

Flats and trainers

Look for pedals with a broad platform and plenty of grip. You can use any kind of shoe with this type of pedal if you are

Riding with trainers.

just nipping to the shops or cruising round town but for the best experience we'd suggest a cycling specific skate-style shoe with a tacky sole which will help your foot grip the pedal and a stiff sole for better energy transfer.

Commuting and touring shoes

If you are likely to be hopping off your bike to walk into your office, stop in a cafe or mooch about town then SPD pedals and touring shoes are the best compromise between performance and casual styling. The cleat is inset into the sole of the shoe so you are able to walk around easily but you still have the benefit of being able to clip into your pedals. There is a huge range to choose from; you can buy sandals, traditional leather shoes, and ones that look like trainers or even super stiff carbon soled mountain bike shoes.

Road shoes

Road shoes are for out and out performance; they are hard to walk around in because of the large cleat on the bottom which walking will damage. The soles are very stiff and smooth for optimal power transfer so whilst they perform amazingly while you are on the bike off the bike you are in danger of looking like Bambi on ice as you skitter around in them. These are perfect for long distance rides where you only expect to unclip your feet a few times and will not need to walk anywhere.

Commuting shoes (above) and road shoes (right).

Choosing your pedal set-up

'The problem I had occurred when I changed pedal set-up, moving from Look D type to Keo pedals. The right cleat was turning my heel in towards the frame, which caused the whole leg to be slightly twisted. Not noticeable if you are riding occasionally, but it started to cause severe pain and inflamed the tendons in the knee area. Therefore a trip to the doctors was required. I moved the cleat and followed up with a two-week course of anti-inflammatories. For first timers I would recommend using floating cleats rather than fixed to allow for a margin of error. The best way is to either set things up on a turbo with a mirror in front of you make sure you look square on the pedals or have someone with a good eye that can make sure that you are square on.'

Garry Russell, 33, Scotland

Setting up your cleats

Cleats clip your foot securely into the pedal so it is really important that they are set up correctly. Over the course of a ride your legs will turn the pedals thousands of times with your knee bending and straightening each time. A misalignment of your cleats can lead to muscular pain in your legs, knees or hips. Many bike shops will fit your cleats for you for a small charge but you can do it yourself by following the steps below.

Most pedals offer some degree of 'float': this is the amount that the cleat can move within the pedal as you press down. This allows your legs some freedom of movement so if your cleats are not set up 100 per cent accurately you can still find a comfortable position. If you have a pre-existing knee injury or you start to develop any niggling pains we'd suggest you ask an expert to help you with setting up your cleats and ask them to check your knee alignment and tracking as you pedal.

Some people can develop a hot burning sensation in the ball of their foot during long rides. Rather simply known as 'hot foot' this is caused by the pressure and pinching of the nerve running between the knuckle of your big toe, as you constantly press down on the pedals, particularly if using shoes with stiff soles. One way to alleviate this is to use a shoe with a 'metatarsal button' such as Specialized's Body Geometry range. It works by lightly lifting and spreading the toes, alleviating the pinching of the nerve.

1 Sit on the edge of a table and let your legs swing naturally. Observe if your toes turn in or out. This is most likely to be the position you need to feel comfortable when pedalling.

2 Put your shoe on and feel for the ball of your foot, the base of your big toe, on through the shoe. Find where it is and using masking tape to protect your shoe make a small mark.

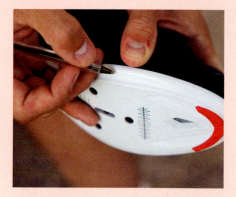

3 Find the base, the first 'knuckle' of your little toe and again make a mark on the outside of your shoe.

4 Loosely fix the cleat to the bottom of the shoe and then move it up or down until the horizontal centre of it is between the two marks you made on your shoe.

5 Angle the cleat so that it mimics the angle of your feet when hanging off the table, if you are unsure then fix them straight and allow the float in the pedals to allow you to find the right spot once you are riding.

6 Make sure you tighten up the cleat before you try them in the pedals. Go for a short ride to test that your knees and feet feel in a natural position.

5

Building fitness

While this book isn't for the next Tour de France racer, it's good to have something to strive for. And the great thing is, it doesn't matter what you choose as it's totally up to you.

Cycling is what you make it and who are we or anyone else to say otherwise? In this book we're not going to tell you to do this or that, or introduce you to using structured plans if that's not what you want to do.

Many cyclists quickly get disheartened when they don't reach the targets that they set out some months before. But what a lot of these cyclists find is that these weren't the goals that they initially set out to achieve, and somewhere along the line, the goal has changed. If your target, goal, aim or whatever you want to call it doesn't come from you initially, then you'll never stick to it.

While it's very important to have a clear target in mind, and a realistic plan of how to 'get there,' there's absolutely no harm in just getting out and riding your bike. A lot of people get too fixed up on goal setting, and it can become an obsession. If you have a plan, then great, but make sure you follow it. If you don't, then fine. Just get out and ride.

Getting started

Sometimes, getting started is the hardest part. It can be quite daunting heading out on your own through the city streets or along country lanes.

Someone always has a horror story of a ride from hell, which they seem to have a delight in telling you. It's enough to put you off the thought of riding a bike forever. But it's important to remember these stories are rare, and, in almost every case, they are exaggerated.

If you are worried about heading off onto the roads – a lot of people are, so don't feel like you're on your own – try and find a friend who will ride with you. If there isn't anyone, then head out for 15 minutes or so, around the block where you live just to get used to riding on your own.

Cycling is all about building, brick by brick. Start off small, and slowly increase with each week and each ride.

Turn that 15-minute ride into a half hour one. Next weekend, try and get out for a whole hour. It may seem all a bit insignificant when compared to someone else who is out riding their bike for entire days at the weekends, but everyone is different, whether that be cycling experience, ability or fitness.

Getting fitter

In terms of fitness, it's very important to not overdo it from the word go. Stay within your limits, and enjoy what you are doing first. That's the most important thing.

If you enjoy it, as with anything else, you are much more likely to do it again. Going out for a massive ride, which rips your legs to pieces, when you're not physically ready, isn't going to make you want to jump straight back on the bike, is it?

Cycling isn't hard, nor should it be daunting, providing you use your brain. OK, watching Sir Chris Hoy boom himself round the track at a zillion miles an hour is scary, but thankfully, all you have to do is watch him, and marvel at his talent and ability.

For you guys, especially those who are just starting out, begin slowly and build your base fitness. Over time, your fitness levels will improve, your legs will feel stronger and you will be able to ride for longer. It is then when you can start to look toward bigger challenges.

Think of your fitness as a pizza. It sounds stupid doesn't it? But hear us out. If you want to make your own pizza, you wouldn't start by chucking on the toppings, would you? No, you'd make the base first. Think of this as your core fitness. Get this 'done' before you start adding your toppings, which will be your higher end fitness. The bigger you want to make your pizza and your fitness, the bigger the base must be. See, it does make sense, sort of.

Setting goals

Goals are handy things to have. While it can make everything feel a lot more formal, they will help. There are a number of reasons why people set goals; it could be for charity or even for a personal achievement, but the reason they are set, is to help stick to it and keep some structure.

Riding as and when you want to is fantastic. And it's great to have that freedom to ride when you like but if you are truly keen on getting fit, and/or reaching a specific target within a certain time frame, then it's good to have a goal.

Once again, these could be absolutely anything; a sportive, an all day ride, a charity event or even a cycling holiday that you want to take in the middle of the summer.

Some cyclists like the idea of actually signing up to something, and even paying an entry fee. For many people financial input and an end goal will really help you to stick with it, as you know when it is, and what you will have to do to complete it. Not only that, but if you don't do it, you've wasted your hard earned money.

A cycling holiday is a great goal to have as well, whether that's in the south of France or Cornwall. Not only are you more likely to get out and ride each weekend in preparation for your holiday; the fitter you become, the more you will enjoy your holiday.

A goal is a target, that you believe you have to work towards in order to achieve it. Remember it can be anything. It's your goal and no one else's.

The easier it gets

The best thing about cycling, is that the more you do, whether it's road riding, mountain biking, on your BMX, gym spinning or on a Boris Bike around London, the fitter you get, the easier it becomes. And the fitter you become, the more fun there is to be had.

You can ride further, you can ride faster, you can try new longer, challenging routes, you can enter events, you can try other bikes and styles or you could even join a cycling club and meet like-minded people.

Without sounding cheesy, the list is endless and the more you ride, the more you will be able to do.

But it's not just about getting fit and healthy. Cycling can do so much more. It can help bring people together, create a sense of worth, build relationships, reduce stress and depression, improve immunity, increase productivity and change your way of life. Don't believe us? Well read and you see for yourself.

Planning your routes

You've got a bike and you're ready to go but where to ride it? The criteria for choosing a route for your bike ride are different to planning an A–B journey or going somewhere in your car. We explore the options and look at what makes a great cycle ride.

A bike gives you the freedom to go anywhere: you could pedal away from your house intending to nip to the shops, ride to a cafe, head for the coast or ride around the world. Each journey starts the same way: you just put your feet on the pedals and go! How you plan that route is very much down to each individual, some people are happy to follow their noses and sniff out adventures along the way where as others prefer the security of having a set route planned out.

How to choose a route

When they first start cycling many people stick to routes they know from driving. This means you are missing out on the huge diversity of cycle paths, quiet lanes and roads that have become almost traffic-free once bypasses or faster dual carriageways have been built. It's not unusual to see a cyclist on a busy main road being battered and windblown by passing lorries, unaware that just over the hedge or across the field there is the 'old' road running virtually parallel to where they are riding but with no traffic on it at all. The only way to spot these routes is by looking at a map.

There are lots of tools and resources for planning routes in the next few pages but the first thing you have to think about, even before you get out your map or GPS, is what you want to get out of your ride. A commute to work needs to be fairly direct, safe and as enjoyable as possible. When planning a single day's ride you might want to meander in and out of quiet routes, taking in a few challenging hills or particularly scenic areas. It doesn't matter how much that route wiggles and twists because however far you go you will still end up at your door.

If one of your fears is getting lost on a ride then investing in a GPS cycle computer can be invaluable. It makes navigation very easy and, if all else fails, you can normally just hit the 'go-home' function!

The National Cycle Network

Sustrans' National Cycle Network covers 14,000 miles of walking and cycling routes. These routes make use of quiet roads, scenic traffic-free paths, signed on-road routes and long distance routes so there is something for everyone.

Sustrans was founded in Bristol in 1977 and the first path was the Bristol and Bath Railway path, a 17-mile traffic-free trail along a disused railway. The Network was officially created in 1995 with a grant from the newly created National Lottery. It now carries over a million walking and cycling journeys daily and passes within a mile of 57 per cent of the population. Look out for the blue signs near you.

Visit www.sustrans.org.uk to view their interactive map or visit their shop where they sell maps of routes and many regional guidebooks.

The most popular UK cycle routes

Within the UK there are many well-trodden, or rather well-wheeled, cycle routes many of which are sign-posted and have accompanying maps and guidebooks. Other than London to Brighton all of the routes below make perfect multi-day trips for a relaxing holiday or could be the inspiration for a single day ride. As they are so popular there are many holiday companies offering fully supported and guided trips so you have nothing to worry about except enjoying the view, alternatively you can pack up your panniers and do it under your own steam.

Land's End to John O'Groats

There are numerous ways to cycle between the two furthest extremities of our island but no set route or sign-posted cycle trail. You'll find a wealth of books and resources are available with detailed route guides offering all manner of possibilities from the traditional 874 mile route to those offering the most scenic and quiet of roads. If you want to get an overall perspective on the diversity of food, culture and terrain the UK offers this is a perfect way to do it.

C2C – Sea to Sea

The UK's most popular signed cycle route this was designed by Sustrans and is part of the National Cycle Network. The route runs from Whitehaven to Tynemouth or Workington and crosses the Lake District and Peninnes. It has been designed to be suitable for riders of all abilities and uses a variety of disused railway lines, minor roads and specially constructed cycle paths. It is 140 miles long and can be done over several days with lots of options for overnight stops. Between 12,000 and 15,000 cyclists ride it every year.

London to Brighton

There are multiple charities offering organised versions of London to Brighton including the original British Heart Foundation event but it is a popular route for riders living in the south-east all year round. As with Lands End to John O'Groats there is no set or sign-posted route but it is well documented on line with GPX files available to down load.

Hadrian's Wall Cycle Way

Sustrans route 72 stretches the entire length of Hadrian's Wall; it offers magnificent coastal views, beautiful countryside and Roman forts. The ride combines a great sense of history with inspirational rural riding. It's 174 miles long and fully sign-posted and makes full use of country lanes and cycle paths so you can relax and enjoy the dramatic

On-line resources

www.Mapmyride.co.uk *Offering far more than just mapping this site allows you to log your workouts, keep track of your mileage, plan and share routes with your friends and it even has a food diary and journal. If you are cycling for improved fitness this has everything you need to help you record your progress. Its mapping function is easy to use and you can create or search for routes in any area of the world you choose.*

www.bikehike.co.uk *A free website run on donations from users to provide UK cyclists with access to Ordnance Survey maps. This is a fantastic resource for planning any off-road adventures as it shows bridleways, byways and footpaths not available on general road mapping. You can add way markers, find out the elevations of your route and upload directly to your Garmin GPS unit.*

www.endomondo.co.uk *Endomondo is a free on-line community where you can share routes with other cyclists and runners all over the world. If you are going somewhere new or just want a different route in your own local area then it is easy to look up and down load routes that have been designed by other cyclists.*

countryside. There is easy access to a range of public transport at both start and end points and plenty of accommodation options along the way.

Way of the Roses

Running between Morecambe and Bridlington the 170-mile route takes riders through some of the most beautiful parts of Yorkshire Wolds and Dales, as well as passing many historical sites associated with the War of the Roses including the beautiful cities of York and Lancaster. Made up of traffic free paths, cycle lanes and quiet country lanes it is well sign-posted in both directions.

West Country Way

Although it makes use of Sustrans Route 3, the West Country Way was designed by two cyclists who enjoyed their holiday experience so much they decided to share it with other people. Running from Bristol to Padstow – or vice versa – the route shows off much of the stunning scenery of the West Country. It takes in the high hedgerowed Cornish lanes and traffic-free cycle routes such as the Tarka Trail. It is 250 miles long and follows paths in the Mendips, along the North Devon coast and Exmoor National Park.

Sat-nav for bikes

Once you have plotted a route on-line it is time to upload to a handle bar mounted GPS. There are many GPS bike computers on the market offering a range of sophistication and a few extra tricks to keep you entertained on the road. Expect to spend anything from £70 to £400 depending on the extra functions you desire beyond simple mapping and navigation.

The Cyclists' Touring Club

The Cyclists' Touring Club was founded in 1878, today they are involved in all kinds of cycling related charity work and campaigning from fighting for justice for cyclists or families affected by road traffic accidents through to sorting out pot holes and clearing cycle paths. They also offer a wide variety of cycle training schemes for adults and are an excellent resource for route planning and advice. Their website offers a journey planner and access to maps and routes created by their members. www.ctc.org.uk

Cycling safely

How to be a safe cyclist

Although we all hope to experience respect from other road users it's important to take steps to make yourself as safe as possible when you're out on your bike.

It's not just urban settings where you need to think about your safety, we look at all the potential hazards and how having your wits about you will help you to cycle with confidence in every scenario.

Which lights for me?

When you're caught out leaving work a little late, or you stay in the pub longer than you anticipated, back-up lights that you can chuck in your rucksack and easily fit onto your bars or seat post are a godsend. Brands such as Knog and Cateye provide solutions that stretch round any handle bar, with no need for additional fixtures.

However for regular journeys or if you have sections of your commute on poorly-lit lanes you will want to consider a heavy-duty front light which will cost a bit more and tend to come with remote battery packs that you recharge over night. These can be as bright as a car headlamp and will mean that drivers have no excuse for not seeing you. What's more they will light your path ahead when you really need it. Brands such as Hope, Lumicycle and Exposure Lights provide popular solutions.

Be safe be seen!

It's important to take all the measures you can to be as visible as possible when you're out cycling on the road. Whether it's day or nighttime, forget vanity and wear as much bright clothing and accessories as you can. Black may be slimming but it won't increase your chances of being noticed.

What's more, when the great British weather is leaving something to be desired the light can be pretty dim even during the daylight hours, so there's never any harm in lighting up like a Christmas tree!

You must always ride with a clear front and red rear light by law but it's your responsibility to ensure that they are positioned where they can be clearly seen, i.e. not covered by a saddle bag or clothing. What's more, sticking an emergency back-up light on for regular journeys isn't enough, the brighter the better and there are plenty of great bike lights available at budget prices so there really is no excuse.

Accessories such as high-viz sashes are great safety additions but if you really are super-style conscious many brands are integrating fluoro and reflective trimming into their clothing designs and bags for a more subtle way to be seen. Subtle on first looks but incredibly effective when they catch a car headlamp. Rucksack covers and bright yellow jackets are also staple items to add to your cycling wardrobe.

Road positioning

As with your clothing choices, the more visible you make your hand signals and intentions on the road the more chance you have of remaining safe. Always have your wits about you and anticipate what motorists and pedestrians are going to do, even if they're in the wrong.

Make a clear arm signal if you intend to move left or right but also use eye contact where possible and always look before you make a move. If someone looks like they are going to pull out or step off the kerb in front of you, look them in the eye to see if they've seen you. Even if you have the right of way it's not uncommon for other road users not to look and you have to make your safety a priority. That said, often the more assertive and confident you are, the less likely you are to be cut up so be clear, and make decisive moves once checking it's safe to do so.

Cycling Instructor and Road Safety Officer Ed Clark explains how taking the 'Primary position' can sometimes be the safest option, noting that every scenario needs to be assessed individually to make the safest choice for you.

Go with the flow

'In heavy traffic, cyclists can benefit from cycling within the flow of traffic. This is often referred to as the 'Primary position'. Cycling within the flow of traffic discourages drivers from overtaking when it is unsuitable or unsafe to do so. It also can allow a cyclist to gain better sight when using or cycling past a junction. By keeping traffic behind them cyclists can make better observations without vehicles obscuring their view and making them less visible to other road users.

'When adopting the primary position, cyclists must think about communication with other road users. By simply making eye contact or using a signal a cyclist can make their movements and intentions clearer to other road users. Poor communication and unpredictable riding can cause conflict between cyclists and other road users.'

Rural riding

When you're riding in more rural environments it's just as important to remain alert. The challenges are different to those you will face in rush-hour traffic but your safety is still just as important.

You may not see another vehicle for hours on end if you're out for a potter in the lanes, which is great but can lure you into a false sense of security. If you're hitting a downhill section, take it with caution and watch out for tractors pulling out of fields or dogs off their leads that may run in your path.

For example, if a squirrel makes a beeline for your wheel the worst thing you can do is jam your brakes on full and risk going over the handlebars. Remain calm and try to anticipate where it's going to go, don't panic, the chances are it will run in the other direction and you'll avert disaster without having to make an emergency stop! Similarly if you see wet leaves up ahead, gently ease off your pace and roll over them without hitting the brakes.

Potential road hazards

Diesel in the road or ice in the winter can make for tricky ground to cover but by looking up the road ahead and trying to anticipate what's coming up you should be able to give potential hazards a wide berth. Keep your eyes peeled and if you do find yourself on any slippery stuff, again, the last thing you should do is brake over it. Keep your body relaxed, maintain a straight line and roll over, make no sudden movements and you should clear things with no problem.

If you are cycling within a group it's friendly to point out potential hazards such as parked vehicles, large potholes or slippery drain covers. When you're focusing on keeping up with the rider in front you may not be able to see what's on the ground so it will help keep the whole group upright!

Another issue that can occur when cycling in a large group is the need to make a sudden stop, because the last thing you want is to plough into the wheel in front. A simple arm in the air will show others that you intend to stop. However, if you are nervous removing your hand from the bars, simply shout to the group that you are 'stopping!' Communication is key.

Danger zones

Bike lanes may seem like a safety zone but sadly you will often find vehicles parked in them, gaping pot holes and drivers pulling in past the line. For this reason you need to be just as careful when using them and keep your eyes up ahead, don't assume you won't come across any obstacles!

The more you ride the more you'll become familiar with common danger zones to look out for, for example, pedestrians stepping off the bus and simply walking out in front of you without looking. Again, although it's your right of way, cover the brakes just in case!

Car doors opening out on you are another potential peril and so look out for signs such as someone being in the driver seat or the wing mirror being folded out when the others are folded in. If it looks like someone may open a door, check over your shoulder and if safe, pull out past the car with enough room so that if the worst happens you can avoid it.

Our golden rule is to err on the side of caution. As much as we hope people drive with due care and attention, cyclists are more vulnerable than those protected by the shell of a car, and so if something seems risky, simply don't do it. If you are in doubt about moving up the inside a vehicle, or getting through a gap in time, just don't do it.

HGVs and bikes: the rules

Ed Clark gives us the lowdown on sharing the road with HGVs: 'When passing a HGV, cyclists must think about their own visibility with regards to the driver. HGV drivers rely on their mirrors to see behind them, so if a cyclist cannot see the vehicle's mirrors, they should assume that the driver does not know that they are there.

'Cyclists should avoid undertaking HGVs. When undertaking, a cyclist will have limited space between the pavement and the vehicle. If the vehicle were to drift left this space will become less and leave the cyclist very little options as to where to go. There is also a chance that the vehicle may turn left into a side road across the pathway of a cyclist. To reduce the risk when passing a HGV, the cyclist should overtake the vehicle. This should be done when a cyclist is moving faster than the flow of traffic and there is the appropriate space to do so. If a cyclist is unsure or unconfident of overtaking the best thing to do would be to wait or queue behind the HGV in view of the driver's mirrors.'

Personal safety

We've looked at all the steps you can take to build your confidence in traffic and when you're planning your routes from A to B, but personal safety is another aspect to consider.

Be prepared

By carrying all of the essential items you need to be self-sufficient on general rides and daily commutes you'll ensure you can be on your way quickly in the event of a mechanical failure. For example, in the albeit rare event of a double puncture, failing to carry two spare tubes could mean you walking home in the dark, or being stranded by the road side. Tyre levels, tubes and a mini-pump will prevent this minor glitch affecting your safety.

Don't go off the radar

Tell someone that you're riding home at night, carry a mobile phone and avoid riding poorly lit down back streets or alleys. In the event of anything going wrong with the bike you don't want to be too far off the beaten track.

Light up

If you're riding off road or on country lanes in the winter, invest in some heavy duty lights to enable you to see the path ahead. When you're away from streetlights the last thing you want is for your light to run out of battery or not allow you to see hazards in front of you. Position a main light and a back up light so that you can see potholes or other hazards.

Don't switch off

Awareness of what's going on around you is crucial for personal safety. Sticking headphones in and blasting out the music may be fun but not on the bike. It will impair your judgement as you won't be able to hear the traffic around you and are also more likely to become distracted.

The law

The drink/drive limit as defined by the Road Traffic Act 1988 section 11, only applies to drivers. For cyclists, the test is whether or not they are fit to ride. The Road Traffic Act 1981 section 30 says:

Cycling when under influence of drink or drugs
(1) A person who, when riding a cycle on a road or other public place, is unfit to ride through drink or drugs (that is to say, is under the influence of drink or a drug to such an extent as to be incapable of having proper control of the cycle) is guilty of an offence. (2) In Scotland a constable may arrest without warrant a person committing an offence under this section. (3) In this section 'road' includes a bridleway.

Drink riding

Riding to the pub may keep you fit but keep an eye on what you're drinking. You may not actually be breaking the law but have one too many and you're more likely to put yourself in danger. If you're planning to go out on the lash leave the bike at home, in the office or bring a heavy-duty lock and get the train home! Better to be safe than sorry.

Bike insurance

If you've invested any sort of money in a bike, it makes common sense to look after it. And we don't mean just from dirt and grime, but from pesky thieves.

Bike thefts are a common problem in the UK. In 2011/12, more than 115,000 bikes were reported stolen in the UK (according to stats.stolen-bikes.co.uk).

It's not hard to see why crooks are targeting bikes. Even average bicycles nowadays are worth far more than televisions, computers and laptops. According to the British Cycling Economy report, the average cost for a recreational cyclist is £250, while the cost of an average enthusiast's bike is £1200.

Now this wouldn't be a problem, but ask yourself this: where do you keep your bike each night – the shed, perhaps the garage or even the porch? Don't laugh, some people do.

It's crazy when you think about it. You would never leave your laptop, which costs half as much money in the unlocked shed, would you? Yet each night, hundreds and hundreds of cyclists pack their bikes away, down the back of the garden, with a sign reading 'robbers welcome.'

And thefts aren't just occurring during the dead of night. They are lifted off the back of cars, outside shops, down the park, you name it, wherever a thief can get a chance to nick a bike that isn't secured, they will take it. And you must be aware of that.

Keeping your bike safe

Luckily, there are a few things you can do, to keep your bike safe and the thieves at bay.

Park it in view: Lock and leave your bike in a well lit, busy area where people are constantly passing. A thief is far less likely to try and steal a bike where others are. Locking it up next to a lamppost in a quiet road or beside an alleyway is only asking for trouble.

Lock it up: It only takes a second to steal a bike, so make sure you lock it up at all times. Invest in a good quality D-lock. A poor lock can easily be broken or sawn through. And without wanting to sound patronising, make sure you lock your bike to something immovable.

Even at home, lock it up: The majority of bicycle thefts come from the home. If you can't leave it in your house, make sure that where you leaving it, is secure. And remember to lock your bike up as well. The harder it is for the thief the more likely they are to give up.

Insurance: While it isn't a legal requirement, it certainly makes sense to insure something that is quite costly and can easily be stolen. There are a number of ways you can insure your bike. A common way is through home contents insurance, but there are now many specialist companies now, who offer insurance solely for your bike against theft and damage. If your bike is particularly expensive, then it's worth getting specific insurance. Velosure is just one of a number of companies that offer a service such as this.

Register your bike: Immobilise is the UK's national property register. It's quick, easy to do and very effective. The service is free and can be used my members of the public and police force to trace owners of lost and stolen property. According to www.immobolise.com, 'As a direct result of Immobilise there are over 250 cases a week where property is returned or information collected that assists the Police in investigating criminal activity involving stolen goods.'

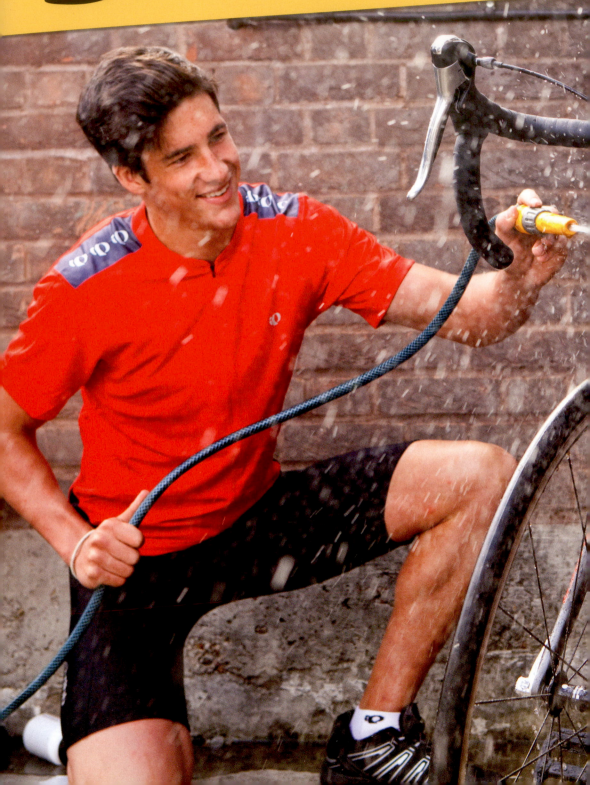

Bike maintenance

7

Look after your bike

The 'M' check

Most things that go wrong with a bike can be prevented by early maintenance. This doesn't mean that you have to become a proficient home mechanic but by learning to do a basic safety check of your bike you are less likely to have problems when you are out for a ride and your bike shop will be able to make any minor repairs before they become more expensive problems.

It may sound odd but learn to listen to your bike. A well maintained bike should run almost silently; any squeaks, creaks or rattles generally means that there is a problem.

The 'M' check is a quick and simple way to ensure you check every part of your bike and nothing gets over looked. Ideally you should do it before every ride; with practice it only takes 2–3 minutes. It will also help you to learn the names of the different parts of your bike, which can help considerably when explaining to a bike mechanic where the problem lies. See below for how to do it.

Saddle · Head-set · Brake levers · Seat post · Top tube · Seat tube · Handle bar · Brake callipers · Down tube · Rear mech · Rim · Front mech · Quick release lever

Bike maintenance checklist

Wheel: Check quick release skewer is firmly closed or that axle nuts are fully tightened.

Tyre wear: Lift the bike to spin each wheel in turn, check that tyres are not split or cracked, look for glass or flints, check the wear of the tread.

Tyre pressure: Check that the tyre is firmly inflated to the recommended pressure on the tyre wall.

Hub bearings: Grip the wheel and rock side to side to feel for loose bearings. Spin the wheel to make sure it runs smoothly.

Rims and spokes: Look for bent spokes or cracks in the rim, spin the wheel to check that it is not buckled.

Brakes: Check angle of levers and that they can be comfortably reached. Apply the brakes one at a time and try to push your bike forward to check they work properly.

Brake blocks: Check that blocks are correctly positioned and plenty of pad remains

Brake cables: Check that cables are not frayed or heavily corroded.

Handlebars stem alignment: Hold front tyre between knees and turn gently to check that the handlebar stem is correctly aligned with the front wheel and tightened.

Handlebar alignment: Check that handlebars are correctly aligned and secured by the stem.

Headset bearings: Apply brakes and rock bike back and for to feel for loose headset bearings; lift front end of bike by the head tube and check that handlebars move freely.

Gears and transmission: Check that chain is lubricated, not heavily rusted.

Saddle: Check that the 'minimum insertion' marker is not visible above the seat tube; check that the post is securely gripped in the frame. Try to rock saddle in different directions to check that it is fitted securely; check that the saddle is sitting straight and level.

Rear mech position: Lift the back end of the bike and spin the rear wheel, check the mech doesn't touch the spokes, look for any damage.

Peripherals: Check that all additional items such as lights, mudguards, racks and any brackets are firmly secured.

Tools you need at home

1 Track pump with gauge It is much easier to get high pressures into your tyres with this than with a mini-pump

2 Ball-ended Allen key set Multi-tools are great for emergency repairs but having separate tools at home makes maintenance jobs much easier.

3 Chain splitter Again the chain splitter on your multi tool will do at a pinch when you are out but a more heavy duty one for home makes light work of changing a chain.

4 Phillips and flat blade screwdriver There aren't many bike parts that require screwdrivers but most homes will have these vital tools anyway.

5 15mm pedal spanner Pedals can become quite difficult to remove so the added leverage of a pedal spanner will make life a lot easier. Just be very careful when putting pedals on to just nip them up, you don't need to put all your force into tightening them.

Things you can do at home

Pump up your tyres

Invest in a decent track pump with a pressure gauge so that you can check your tyres before every ride. The recommended pressure is normally written on the tyre wall. Keeping your tyres at the correct pressure will help reduce rolling resistance so you go faster for less effort and make you less likely to puncture.

Clean and oil your chain

You don't have to keep all of your bike sparkly and clean but the moving parts of the drive train do need a regular check to prevent irritating squeaks, broken chains or increased friction which will slow you down. Degrease your chain regularly, wipe it down and use a good quality cycle lubricant that will stay on the chain and keep it clean.

Change your brake pads

Changing your brake pads is a fairly simple job once you have been shown how to do it. Ask in your bike shop for advice on how to do it. Keep a supply of spare pads at home. Running your pads too low will stop your from braking quickly and efficiently and could cause damage to your rims or brake callipers.

Change your bar tape

This is a purely aesthetic fix but clean bar tape makes your entire bike look better. Changing your bar tape is a simple task that just requires a little bit of patience and neatness. Follow the instructions on page 93 or alternatively here are numerous YouTube demonstrations that you can follow.

On the road repairs

Riding on your own and exploring new areas is one of the simple pleasures of being a cyclist. But many new cyclists worry about what would happen if something went wrong with their bike or they had a puncture as, unfortunately, there is no friendly AA or RAC man available for cyclists. If your bike is generally well maintained and you check it over before you leave home there are actually very few things that are likely to go wrong. The most common one is a puncture which, with a bit of practice and the right tools, everyone can fix for themselves. Ask at your local bike shop or cycling club about basic mechanic lessons where you will be able to practise under expert supervision.

Your on-the-road kit

Below, we set out the basic things to carry with you on a ride either in a small pack that fits under your saddle, in a pannier or in your rucksack. It's well worth playing around with your bike at home or under the supervision of someone from your bike shop so if something happens when you are out you will be able to fix it without feeling flustered. Even if you aren't entirely confident in using the tools and repair kits listed below it is still worth carrying them as other cyclists are nearly always generous with their help so flag down the next rider that passes.

Rarely something might happen that you can't fix on your own, in the absolute worst case scenario it's time to phone a friend, or a taxi, and get a lift back for yourself and your bike. Always carry your phone and some cash as even the most experienced of cyclists have found themselves in situations where the only solution is to get a lift home.

What to carry

<u>Inner tube x 2:</u> Always carry two tubes, if you puncture early on in a ride will be in the position of doing the remainder of the ride without a spare if you only carry one tube.

<u>Patch kit:</u> If you hit a run of bad luck two inner tubes might not be enough so carry back up.

<u>Tyre levers:</u> Unless you have very strong thumbs it is worth carrying levers to make it easy to take your tyre off.

<u>Mini-pump:</u> Small and lightweight these pumps will get enough air into your tyre to get you home safely.

<u>Multi-tool:</u> Everything thing you need for tightening, adjusting or fixing your bike.

<u>Chain splitter:</u> If you snap your chain then you will need a chain splitter to remove the damaged link.

Joining link: These links make re-joining your chain a simple task.

Tyre boot: If you slice open your tyre an old piece of tyre can be placed between the inner tube and the cut to help get you back on the road.

Fixing a puncture

1 Undo the quick-release lever and brake, remove the wheel. Fully deflate the tyre.

2 Stretch the tyre round the rim until there is some slack.

3 Use your tyre levers to hook under the bead and remove the tyre.

4 Check the tyre for thorns or glass remembering to be careful of your fingers. Check the rim.

5 Apply a patch to the damaged area.

6 Slightly inflate the new tube and put it into the tyre

7 Push the tyre back onto the bead being careful not to pinch the inner tube.

8 Re-inflate the tyre.

9 Put the wheel back into your bike and secure the quick release lever and then re-set your brake.

Cleaning your bike

There's nothing better than riding a shiny, clean bike and while it won't make you ride any faster, there's something about riding on something that glistens in the sunlight that makes you want to pedal that little bit harder.

There is also a practical element for having a dirt free bike, other than vanity. Muck and grime will affect your components, which increase the chances of mechanicals when out on the road. A dirty drive train for example, will also work far less efficiently.

It can be hard keeping your bike clean. After a long ride, the last thing on your mind is to go and clean your bike, especially if you've been out in the wind and rain. But try and conjure up the effort, as putting it off will only make things worse.

Mud and grit has a way of finding its way into every nook and cranny, and once it dries, it can be very tricky to remove. So it's important to wash away the grime before it settles. It will also be far easier and quicker.

Do it properly

If you are going to clean your bike, you might as well do it properly. Otherwise you're just wasting your time. Many cyclists believe a quick wash down with a hose will do the trick, but in actual fact, it won't do much. Even if it is a jet hose!

Don't ignore the things you can't see.

Bits & bobs

For example, under the saddle, around the seat cluster and the back of the rear derailleur.

It's worth having some bike cleaning essentials on hand to call upon after every ride. Keep a selection of brushes, baby wipes, sponges, cloths, spray on degreaser and lube in a bucket, stored away in the shed or garage away from everything else. There's nothing more frustrating than spending ten minutes or so in wet cycling gear, on tired legs, trying to find where you left the sponges or degreaser.

No one enjoys cleaning grime off a bike, so the quicker and easier it is done, the better.

Chain

If you want, you can make your own degreaser; one cup of hot water, ¼ cup of liquid soap, two tablespoons of vinegar and ½ teaspoon of washing soda is effective and cheap.

However, if you can't be bothered with that, there are spray-on degreasers on the market that work brilliantly.

Use a small paintbrush with fairly good, stiff bristles and work the degreaser into the chain on both sides, with the chain in the big ring.

Turn the cranks and work along the leading edge of into each chain link, working away from the chain set.

Chain rings

Use degreaser and make sure you get to the teeth and remember to work on the inside chain ring, as this is the part that often gets ignored.

Work the brush into the rear sprockets, pushing it down into the cassette as you whizz the pedals around.

Hold the end of the brush against the jockey wheels as they turn, use a tiny amount of degreaser and avoid the bearing sides if you can.

To remove water from the chain, whizz it around by turning the cranks and then apply lube once it is dry.

A few drops of a medium weight oil on exposed cable guides and on brake pivots and derailleurs will keep them working smoothly.

Wheels

Don't forget about the wheels. Giving the rims a good clean will protect the break pads from harmful deposits that could damage the braking surface.

Wash the tyres too; once clean, it will be much easier to make checks for cuts and embedded shards that could cause punctures. Sponge off any dirt from the hubs and spokes.

Upgrades

When you first buy your bike the chances are you'll love it with all your heart but this can start to wane when you've ridden it for a while. The grease can start to mount, the brand new parts will stop glistening and you may start to lose interest. However, a well maintained bike can look as good as new, so make sure you don't neglect your steed as the months go on.

A good clean after any grimy ride will keep things shiny but also ensure that you keep things well maintained so that the moving parts keep moving.

When it comes to looks and comfort, fresh bar tape, a new saddle or a tyre change can transform your machine.

Grubby bar tape doesn't look good, so spruce things up with a new colour. It's a cheap and cheerful way to brighten up the look of the bike and quick and easy when you know how.

The right tyres for your needs

Over time your tyres will pick up tiny slits and cuts, which eventually could allow grit or glass to work in and potentially puncture the tube. Keep an eye on this and if you're constantly experiencing flats it's probably time to invest in a new set of rubbers. Look out for what suits you, because there's no point in buying race lights if you're going to be using them for winter commuting. What you save in weight will often mean you're constantly puncturing, if you have heavy duty requirements look for a heavier duty tyre. The good news is that there are plenty of options available that combine a relatively light weight with sufficient puncture proofing.

A more comfortable saddle

The chances are you may want to change the saddle from the one your bike was sold with. If you're not fussy it may be that you get along with the standard seat fine but it's such a personal preference that some riders will want to change to a slimmer or wider fit for their seat bones.

Most major bike shops will be able to help you if you go in and ask for saddle advice by sitting you on a memory foam pad and letting you know the best design for you. You may look like you have wide hips but in fact have a small sit bone width, and vice versa so it's worth checking. Women may want to switch to something with more ladylike design attributes!

Fitting handlebar tape

Start at the bottom of the handle bar wrapping in an anticlockwise direction making sure you leave a little overlap; this extra overlap will help secure the bar end in place later.

Once you start moving up the bar, take your time to ensure you leave no bar uncovered, stopping every quarter turn to pull firm. This is to ensure a secure fit whilst eliminating bunching up which can easily be done in the curves of the bar.

When you reach the hoods you will need to place the extra bit of tape usually provided in the tape pack to place directly underneath the lever, pull back the rubber hood covers for better access and allow for the bar tape to sit underneath. With this in place you can continue around the hoods covering the entire handle bar around the levers. Continue until you reach about three to four finger widths from your stem.

To keep a flush look you will need to trim the tape diagonally and use the sticky tape provided to hold into place. Once you are happy with the finished product, place the bar end into the handle bar. Continue the same on other side.

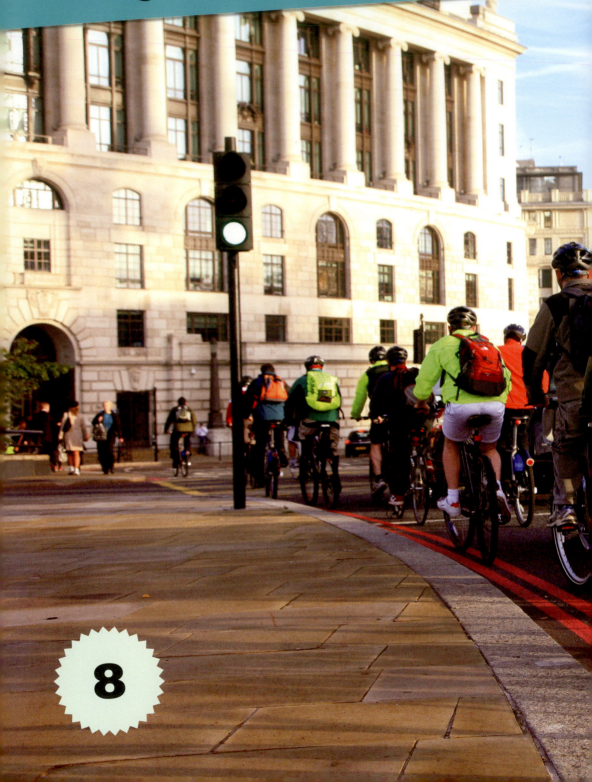

8

Take your bike to work

The Cycle to Work scheme, a UK Government tax exemption initiative, was born in 1999 as part of the Finance Act. It aimed to get more Brits on bikes, promote healthier journeys to work and to reduce environmental pollution.

Essentially, the scheme allows employers to loan bikes and cyclists' safety equipment to employees as a tax-free benefit. The exemption was one of a series of measures introduced under the Government's Green Transport Plan.

It was a dream come true for commuters who could now make significant savings on a new bicycle and pay off the heavily reduced price over a period of 12 months. More commuters were taking to bikes across the UK than ever and cycling was continuing to boom. Employers were starting to enjoy a healthier, more motivated work force and employees were feeling more productive.

In August 2010 Her Majesty's Revenue and Customs (HMRC) issued a statement to clarify the fair market value (FMV) of a bicycle, depending on its original cost, which should be charged if an employee were to take ownership of the bike at the end of the repayment.

Under the scheme you hire the bike, while it still legally belongs to the employer, and then after this clarification from HMRC you would need to pay a percentage of the cost to mark a transaction of FMV. Still with us? Well we wouldn't blame you if you weren't. This caused much confusion in the press at the time, due to the perception that the massive

savings would be diminished. Happily we can report that there are still savings to be made today and you can still get your hands on a brand new bicycle of your choice and pay it off in monthly installments. Even better than that, there are ways around paying the FMV that we'll explain in our FAQs!

The Cycle to Work scheme: the lowdown

What's a salary sacrifice? As defined by HMRC: 'A salary sacrifice arrangement is an agreement between an employer and an employee to change the terms of the employment contract to reduce the employee's entitlement to cash pay. Usually this sacrifice of cash entitlement is in return for some form of non-cash benefit.' In the case of the scheme this non-cash benefit is a new bike.

How do I make savings if I have to pay the money back? This can lower the amount of tax and National Insurance contributions (NICs) your employer deducts and pays to HMRC because the figure on their payroll is the one that is taxable. The savings pass on to you.

Am I eligible to use the scheme? There are some restrictions and so to be eligible you must be paying Pay As You Earn (PAYE), earn more than the National Minimum Wage after salary sacrifice and have a contract that does not end during the hire period. Any company can sign up to the scheme so you'll just need to ask your employer if they are participating in the initiative. Under-18s can join the scheme if their guardian signs a guarantor agreement.

Can I pay off the balance in one go? No. You're essentially hiring the bike from your employer until the end of a typical period of 12 months at which point you have the option of paying the balance and taking ownership of the bike. You can't opt to pay off the balance early, as the minimum hire period is a year.

What happens if the bike is stolen? This responsibility lies with you and if it's stolen, you as the employee would be liable for any outstanding money without any tax exemptions, so you really should get the bike insured straight away. Safety equipment including Home Office-approved Sold Secure D-locks and cable locks can be bought under the scheme.

Does it have to be a certain type of commuter bike to come under the scheme? No. You have a great choice when it comes to the scheme and you can opt for a mountain, hybrid, town, road or folding bike, however the maximum you can spend is £1000 so it must fall in that category.

Can I buy a more expensive bike and pay the difference? No. There used to be an option of a 'top-up' facility, where you could chose the bike of your dreams and pay the difference to the employer, however this produced 'dual ownership' and over-complicated the process so is no longer possible.

What else can I buy under the scheme? Safety equipment is included under the scheme that includes helmets, lights, locks, and high-viz clothing. Whatever you chose to buy must be feasibly used for getting to work so the portion you spend on the bike versus equipment must be realistic.

Can I buy a new bike each year? Yes, as long as you make an agreement with your employer to do so. You are unable to purchase two bikes in one year under the scheme.

How do I avoid paying the full full market value? As you can see in the valuation table opposite, the FMV reduces to next to nothing after five years. There is no obligation to transfer ownership straight away and so the most attractive option for employees is to pay a small, refundable deposit (three per cent or seven per cent of the equipment value) and continue to use the bicycle for an extended period of up to 36 months. Providing your employer agrees to this you can end up saving just as much as you would have done before the new tax rules were introduced.

The valuation table

Age of cycle	Acceptable disposal value percentage	
	Original price less than £500	Original price £500+
1 year	18 per cent	25 per cent
18 months	16 per cent	21 per cent
2 years	13 per cent	17 per cent
3 years	8 per cent	12 per cent
4 years	3 per cent	7 per cent
5 years	Negligible	2 per cent
6 years and over	Negligible	Negligible

Fuel for your ride

The world of sports nutrition can be a rather complex subject, but if you push all the science to one side, the main principles can be broken down quite simply and made easy to understand.

Think of sports nutrition as three sections – before, during and after your ride. You need to fuel up before you go out on your ride, you need to keep the tank topped up during your ride, and then you must replace what you have lost after your ride.

Before

While the body predominantly burns fat for fuel, you will need carbohydrates for when the going gets tough. Luckily the body has quite high fat reserves – even the skinniest of people will have more than enough to last them. However, you only have limited amount of carbohydrate stores. So these need to be stocked up before you head out. Rice, potatoes, white bread, cereals, porridge, these are just a number of the foods that have high concentrations of carbohydrates. If you can, try and get some protein in as well, to help when your ride is over, and fluids.

During

During moderately intense riding, the body will burn around 60g of carbohydrates per hour. These need to be replaced. A pub lunch would do it, as will sport supplements like gels or bars. If you can, try and pack some fig rolls into your jersey, or things like Jaffa Cakes. These will all help in keeping your tank full. And trust us, a full tank is far better than an empty one when you are trying to keep going. It's also important not to ignore your hydration. Keep sipping throughout your ride, even if you're not thirsty as dehydration has a habit of catching up on you.

After

When your ride is over, you need to replace what you have lost: stodge up on carbs and fluids. It's also very important to get a solid amount of protein into your body. Any form of moderate exercise will cause muscle tears, which is also known as muscle trauma. Eating protein soon after exercise will help rebuild your muscles so that they grow back stronger. This in essence is how a body becomes fitter and stronger. If you ignore protein, muscles won't grow, injuries will occur and fitness won't improve. Fail to eat properly after your ride, and you could even get ill.

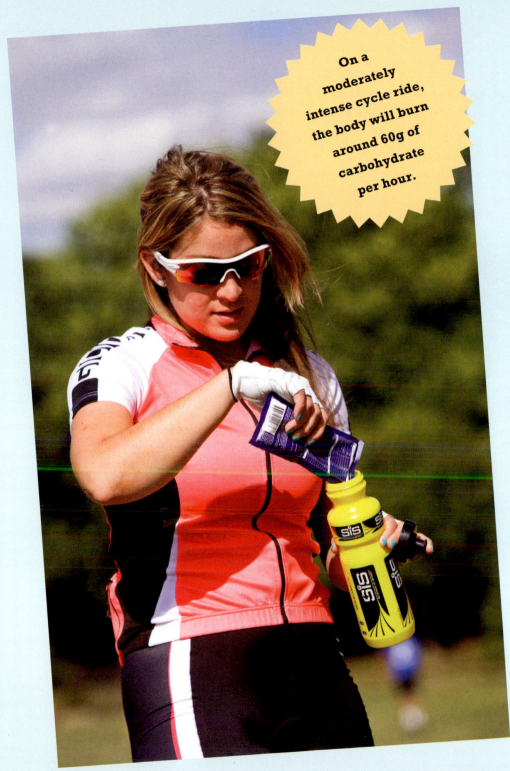

On a moderately intense cycle ride, the body will burn around 60g of carbohydrate per hour.

Getting to work

Riding to work really can change your life. Perks you can expect include having more spare cash, feeling more body confident, increased energy and a clear head.

Once you are in a routine you'll most likely find that commuting by bike saves you time and you'll fit more in than you ever thought possible. Ditch the car, ditch the over-inflated train fares and pedal your way to a healthier, happier you.

It can be daunting when you get started, you lose a shoe, can't locate your bike lights, don't know what the weather is doing or get to work and realise you've forgotten your underwear. However, it only gets better the more you get used to it and find a pattern to your week.

Plan for your ride

Packing a rucksack or pannier the night before will save stress in the mornings and by keeping all your essential riding items together, such as a mini pump, spare tubes and your helmet you'll prevent yourself from forgetting something crucial.

In addition, by adopting a clear routine you won't allow yourself to bail out and the easier you make things for yourself, the more you'll be motivated to get out of the front door and get on your bike.

Carrying your stuff

There are plenty of great storage solutions for cyclists on the market, meaning you can carry anything from a t-shirt to a suit without it becoming creased. However, it's not every day you want to cart all your belongings with you and so leaving bulky items at work is a good solution to lightening your load.

Leave items in the office

Everyone needs a rest day in the week so plan a day to leave the bike at home and take all the things you need in and out of the work place. For example take jackets and shoes in, leave them in the office and then schedule a day to take anything home that needs washing. If you have to be particularly smart for work it's a good idea to keep all your suits in the office and get them dry-cleaned so all you have to think about is cycling kit.

Looking good at work

With the assistance of the Cycle to Work scheme getting a new bike has never been easier. But when it comes to getting on it first thing in the morning many riders are put off from making the switch from car or public transport for a number of reasons. Will I have a beetroot-coloured face all day? Perhaps I'll be too hungry to get through the morning? What if my colleagues laugh at my Lycra or I have nowhere to put my bike? Don't let this stop you, the benefits far outweigh the negatives, trust us, and with a bit of planning it can be a logistical cinch.

Scrub up

Many riders have admitted to us that the initial concern they had when it came to getting on two wheels was the way they would look when they arrived at their destination. Arriving at a nine o'clock meeting sweaty, dishevelled and in Lycra is far from ideal but armed with a few tricks up your sleeve people will never know you've traveled in by bicycle. Well, except for the healthy glow and energy you'll bring with you to that meeting.

Have a recce of your place of work and decide what you need to make the ride in feasible. While you'd ideally want showers and changing facilities you may have to settle for toiletries at your desk and a change of clothes. With a little planning you can freshen up and transform yourself into a picture of composure in no time at all.

Firstly, don't be afraid to ask your employer if there is scope for a shower or whether there are facilities in the building that you could use. You'll be surprised how many other people want to cycle in but feel the same as you.

In the meantime, hand driers can become hair driers and wet wipes an emergency freshen-up in a packet. Buy two sets of essential toiletries and leave them at your place of work so that you don't have to kart everything in each day. Brands such as Muc-Off and Batiste have come up with a shower in a can with their antibacterial 'no water needed' spray and dry hair shampoo, all solutions worth checking out when you're commuting by bike.

Go for low-maintenance looks, such as tying long hair back and keep things simple or keep styling equipment such as straightening irons at your desk.

If you haven't got space to store clothing at work look for lightweight clothing and roll it up to help prevent creasing en route. Have a think about what you want to wear and don't weigh yourself down with things you don't really need.

When it comes to comments from your colleagues you can expect compliments for your new, healthy physique and if there's any negativity they're only jealous!

Avoid overheating

The clothing you choose to wear on the ride in to work can make a huge difference to how you feel when you get there. Dress in breathable fabrics to avoid overheating and similarly if it's wet and windy avoid the chill by covering up.

Snack time

When you start commuting by bike, you'll probably feel more hungry than usual. This is great because you will either start to lose weight, or you get to snack more. Always have healthy snacks with you at work to avoid the hunger knock and to make sure you can get home at the end of the day.

Bike security

The last thing you want when you're busy at work is to be worrying about your bike being stolen. Sadly the reality is that thefts are common so you have to take measures to secure your steed as far as possible. Ask your employer if there is a secure place to lock it up and if not, invest in the best in bike locks, preferably two, register your bike, insure it and make sure it's not left somewhere that allows someone time to cut through the locks and get away with it. See the details on Immobilise on page 81.

Weight loss

9

Get the weight down

The majority of people, especially cyclists, would like to shed a bit more weight. Let's be honest with ourselves, shall we?

And while it's not always much, sometimes it can be a few pound that loiters around the thigh area; it's enough to call a nuisance. Especially when it doesn't seem like it wants to budge.

Now we're not telling you that you have to lose weight, after all, if you're comfortable and happy, then perfect. But if you are one of those people who are struggling to get the weight off and in some cases, keep it off, then perhaps it's worth following some advice.

Losing weight will have a huge impact to your bike riding, no matter what level or ability you are. To put it simply, the less weight you carry, the easier it is to ride your bike.

There are some cyclists who don't believe this is true, and question just how much of a difference it can make. If you are one of those, try going out riding for an hour or so with a heavy backpack on. It's not impossible, but it's uncomfortable enough. Now go out again, without the backpack on. The difference you'll find is quite remarkable, and a heck of a lot easier.

Keeping it going

The thought of losing weight can be quite daunting for some. Many believe the only way to achieve this is to stick to a strict training regimen, live off only rice cakes and celery, and ride hundreds of miles a week. But it needn't be like that, and who would really want it to be like that?

The world isn't an ideal place, and sometimes situations arise where it's impossible to always eat 'right' and get out and exercise as much as one would like. We are all real people with real lives.

There's no denying that many people want to lose weight and become fitter, but wanting and doing are two very separate things. According to UK National Health statistics, obesity levels are on the rise, while weight loss programmes, gym memberships and diet supplement companies are growing in popularity faster than ever. Something does add up.

A clear pattern is emerging; starting your diet and training isn't the hard thing, maintaining it, is.

All in moderation

Diet is a big factor in weight maintenance. In fact, the huge growth of fast food and ready meals has diluted the effect of exercise. It seems cycling isn't enough to keep those unwanted pounds from creeping up on you.

Fast food is no longer seen as a treat, and is becoming the norm. Walk through any town centre, and there will be more fast food stores than there are shops. Meals are no longer seen as a sit down event and people are opting for the easier option of microwave or instant meals.

You must get your diet right, but that doesn't mean you have to go without the things you enjoy. It's all about moderation. Eat right, have the occasional treat, exercise regularly and enjoy yourself.

If you want that chocolate bar, have it, but don't have it everyday. If you fancy a glass of beer or two, then fine. But know when to stop.

Stick to the 80 per cent rule. Get your diet right 80 per cent of the time and you are still likely to be eating a balanced enough diet.

No one should have to forgo the pleasures of life and as long as you exercise frequently enough, and don't go crazy with what you eat, you haven't got to.

Setting goals

Once you have your diet under control (sort of), the next step is to compliment it with your cycling. Get it right, and the weight will start to come down and more importantly, it will also stay off.

As with anything, you must stick with it. Anyone can say they are going to start cycling and lose weight, but the hard part is doing it.

How much exercise do you need to do?

The recommended guideline for the amount of exercise most people should be doing each week is roughly 150 minutes, which in cycling terms, equates to one 40-mile bike ride every weekend.

It's not much is it? And when you break it down, it's actually very little. However, many people struggle, because they can't find the time to spread the 150 minutes out over the week – something health experts have always recommended.

But according to a new study, from Queen's University, Canada, those who accumulated 150 minutes of exercise on a few days of the week were not any less healthy than adults who exercised more frequently throughout the week.

The team of researchers studied 2,324 adults to determine whether the frequency of physical activity throughout the week is associated with risk factors for diabetes, heart disease and stroke.

'The findings indicate that it does not matter how adults choose to accumulate their 150 weekly minutes of physical activity,' says lead researcher, Dr. Janssen. 'For instance, someone who did not perform any physical activity on Monday to Friday but was active for 150 minutes over the weekend would obtain the same health benefits as someone who was doing 20–25 minutes of activity on a daily basis.'

So for those of you how can't find enough gaps in the week to get out and ride, one or two open windows will work just as well.

Make your goal specific

We talked earlier about setting clear targets and goals. Losing weight is a goal. Now it's up to you to make it more specific. The more specific it is, the clearer it is and the easier it will be to follow.

Just saying 'I want to lose some weight' doesn't really mean anything. However, saying 'I want to lose one stone within six months; then breaking it down to 2.5llb every month' is much clearer and easier to plan and adhere to.

Be honest with yourself and work out how high up in the pecking order your request for improved health and fitness actually comes. After work and family commitments, you'll probably find you can fit it in quite high without disrupting your life up too much.

At the start of each week, take a careful look at your diary and plan in advance when and how long you're going to commit to riding your bike in the coming seven days. You may think you are really busy, but you'll be amazed at how much time you can find if you really want to do it.

case study *Cycling and weight loss*

Liam Courtier, 26, lives in Essex and works as a senior estimator for Mobile Shelving and Office Furniture. At his heaviest he weighed 14 stone, 5 pounds and thanks to cycling he's shed the fat to achieve a lean 11 stone, 6 pounds. He tells us what the transformation means to him.

'I had spent years going to the gym and working out but was never happy with my physique or the way I looked. I decided after looking through photos that I wanted to lose weight and slim down. By this point I had also started cycling and was sick of being dropped by my friends because of fitness issues and a weight disadvantage and decided it was time to crack on and focus on getting into shape.

'I had spent roughly three years going to the gym, weight training for six days a week with no cardio at all. As you can imagine I became unbelievably unfit and a lot heavier due to the muscle I was gaining from the weights but I also wasn't burning fat off. Once I decided enough was enough, I started to do spinning classes three times a week during the winter months. Along with this, two evenings a week I began taking part in a class called TFD Insanity Training that I had found out about through a friend. It's basically a full-body workout designed to build stamina and muscle endurance while burning body fat at the same time. This is where I began to get some of my fitness back and get back into good shape.

I decided to get a road bike, firstly because my friend Jack was selling his very nice Specialized Roubaix and I wanted it! And also because I really enjoyed spinning but I didn't want to sit in a gym studio for an hour when I could spend a few hours in the sun working hard on a road bike.

'I knew if I carried on working hard and pushing myself every ride I would get fitter and fitter and at the same time I would be burning fat and losing weight. Over time this happened and I eventually got faster and more powerful on my road bike. This proved to me that the hard work was paying off and I was hooked from then on.

'My physique has changed massively since I started cycling and eating a balanced diet. In the first six months I was keeping a regular check on my weight and I lost 2.5 stone. I am now at a weight and size I am happy with and can maintain fairly easily due to the miles I do on the bike each week. My main goal now is to maintain the same weight but keep increasing my fitness and muscle endurance and power to allow me to improve my average speeds per ride.

'I feel normal, I'm still the same old me except being in good shape gives you confidence and makes you comfortable about doing pretty much anything you like. One of the best things about losing this much weight is having the excuse to completely restock the wardrobe. As a true Essex boy along with most of my mates we live by the fact you have to have look good, which means tans are topped up, your hair is immaculate and your clothes have to fit properly. Our overall look must be 'Lem'!

'The best thing about cycling for me is the fact that it never gets easy, you can spend years doing it and you just push yourself harder and harder the fitter you get so it's never an easy ride. It's a great way to get in shape and get fit and it never get boring because you can just cycle a different route for different challenges.

'I have a lot more energy now that I am cycling often; also, due to the exercise I do my metabolism has reached new levels of speed. I eat a lot more now than I used to and even though I am eating the right foods I am constantly hungry. It's great!'

Nutrition

If you want to lose weight then you are going to have to expend more calories than you put in.

One of the most common mistakes people make when they are trying to lose weight is to skimp on food before or during exercise. This leaves you too hungry to put energy into cycling and can leave you ravenous and likely to binge after you finish your ride. If instead you start your ride properly fuelled and have a few snacks to sustain yourself during long rides you will actually be able to ride further, and a little faster, which will burn more calories. The harder and faster you ride the more calories you burn after exercise as well so under eating, if it means you have to ride more slowly, will mean you miss out not only on extra calorie burn during your ride but after your ride as well.

Pre-ride meal: *porridge or scrambled eggs on wholegrain toast or wholegrain toast with peanut butter*

During your ride: *jelly sweets, bananas, fig rolls, malt loaf, cereal bars,*

After your ride: *milk and a banana, fruit smoothie, tuna jacket potato*

What fuels your body?

There are three main macronutrients that fuel your body: carbohydrate, protein and fat. You need all three to be healthy and have enough energy to support your everyday life and cycling.

Carbohydrate is your body's preferred source of fuel: the snacks you have before and during your bike ride should be predominantly carbohydrate. Fruit and vegetables, cereals, rice, potatoes and pasta are all good sources. Before your rides choose carbohydrate sources that release their energy slowly such as a big bowl of porridge for breakfast. During your ride it's OK to have a few fast releasing carbs such as jelly sweets, as the energy will be quickly burned up by your bike riding.

Protein has many essential roles in your body: it is needed to re-build tissue, for correct hormone function and to maintain your immune system. Protein is made up of 20 different amino acids of which nine are considered to be essential. You need at least 20 per cent of your diet to be protein based. Complete sources of protein can be found in animal based products such as meat, eggs and milk. Vegans and vegetarians have to be a little bit more protein aware but there are plenty of plant-

116

based protein sources that if properly combined give the full range of amino acids. Protein is particularly important after you have been cycling as your body needs to have a source of amino acids to make repairs to muscle tissue; it is an important part of your recovery.

Fat isn't the enemy of weight loss so don't be frightened to include it in your daily diet. The trick is to choose the right kinds of fat. Your diet should contain around 20 per cent fat from healthy unsaturated sources such as cold pressed oils, avocado, oily fish, nuts and seeds. Fat plays an important role in the absorption of vitamins and it is good for your skin, mental function and long-term health.

To lose one pound of body fat a week you need to have a calorie deficit of 3500kcal, that is just 500kcal a day.

Treats and rewards

One of the biggest barriers to weight loss is the urge to reward yourself for your discipline with food or the exercise you have done. We know just how tempting it is, you've done a lovely long ride so treat yourself to a big slab of carrot cake in the cafe at the end. You've eaten really well all day so think that you deserve to splash out on a naughty dessert after dinner. That's fine, part of the reason we love riding our bikes is that it gives us the freedom to indulge a bit and get away with it!

However if you really want to lose weight it is a good idea to find other ways to reward yourself apart from food. Save up and buy some new cycle clothing to flatter your new

slimline physique for example. We know that this doesn't supply the immediate gratification of a chocolate bar after dinner so requires a little extra willpower but the other rewards of feeling good about yourself are absolutely worth it.

No one can manage to be disciplined about food all the time. One handy technique is to have a 'treat' day every week where you can eat whatever you want, no calorie counting and no deprivation. This helps to reset your metabolism if you have been under eating and makes you less likely to want to eat treats every day as you know you can have what you want on that day. Really enjoy it and feel good about having your favourite foods.

The other sneaky side effect of a treat day is that you start to realise your body doesn't feel quite so good after filling it with high sugar and high fat foods so over time you stop wanting them because you realise you feel better on the days that you don't.

Number of calories burnt

60 minutes of cycling at 12-14mph

10 stone = 554

12 stone = 665

14 stone = 776

16 stone = 887

18 stone = 997

Do I need to use energy products?

Carbohydrate drinks, sports gels and energy bars are cleverly marketed and it can leave you thinking that you have to have them whenever you are doing any form of exercise. Energy products are a convenient way of getting in the fuel your body needs for cycling in a form that is easily digestible so they do have their place, however for any ride of less than an hour you will be perfectly fine just drinking water provided you had a good snack or meal before you started. On long leisurely rides water, squash or fruit juice with some of your favourite high carbohydrate snacks such as bananas, jelly sweets or cereal bars will give you all the energy you need. If you decide to take part in events where you will be riding for several hours then it would be worth experimenting with carbohydrate drinks and energy products.

Energy and recovery products can be helpful when you are working hard on the bike. But don't rely on them solely as a source of nutrution.

Healthy mind and body

10

Your mental health

In what is quite a surprising statistic, one in four Brits will experience some kind of mental health problem over the course of a year, with depression affecting one in five.

However, what with so many people being affected by mental health problems, should it be a surprising statistic?

There's no denying that this is still classed as a taboo subject by many, and the fact that not everyone wishes to open up about these kind of issues, ensures it's kept hidden away from everyday conversation.

But if we are to go by the health figures, it means that statistically, we are all likely to know someone who has been affected by this issue.

It shouldn't be hidden away into the shadows. It shouldn't be anything to be ashamed of. The issues should be addressed and dealt with just like any other issue one may experience. And cycling can help.

Identifying when things aren't right

First and foremost, people need to be open, and be able to identify themselves when something isn't right. On the same note, friends, family and colleagues of those experiencing problems must try and be aware, which of course, can be hard.

Depression for example – a common problem and one that affects a lot of people in some way or another – isn't that easy to identify, even if it is you who is experiencing it. So for someone else to spot it, or try and help, can be sometimes impossible.

Is feeling 'down' the first step on the spiralling staircase to depression? Can feelings of dread, panic or frustration be associated with other mental health issues?

Talk about it

The World Health Organization defines depression as, 'a common mental disorder that presents with depressed moods, loss of interest or pleasure, feelings of guilt or low self worth, disturbed sleep or appetite, low energy and poor concentration.'

Despite this definition, it still can be tricky to identify what you are experiencing. That's why it's really important you speak to people. Men find it far more difficult to talk about their feelings than women, and if you do find it uncomfortable talking to a mate, there are always phone lines you can ring.

The Samaritans, MIND and Time to Change are just a number of organisations that are there to help.

Exercise and mood

While talking to someone will have a tremendous positive impact, don't underestimate the power of exercise. In fact, many health experts will advise exercise as an effective treatment. There are a number of reasons for this.

Tiredness and lethargy are two very common symptoms of depression, and can easily develop into something far more serious. In a lot of cases, it can have a knock on effect on not only relationships, but also on your work-life balance.

Regular cycling can help counteract the effects. When we go out to ride our bikes, or partake in any physical activity for that matter, our body will react. The heart will start to beat faster, the lungs will breathe heavier, we'll start to perspire and our body will begin to release hormones.

Adrenaline is one of those hormones, and makes the body feel more alert and awake. It makes you feel alive; it puts your senses on edge and stands you attention. You can feel your body, pumping, wheezing and see it moving. Those who partake in very little activity never get that feeling and tiredness starts to become the norm.

Endorphins are also released, which put the body under a state of euphoria. It's a feeling like no other and can become addictive – a reason why so many people exercise so hard is because they are in search of that bigger buzz.

Pushing your body to a place you never thought it could go can wake you up to the pleasures of exercise. It can give you direction and goals to achieve. Exercise becomes limitless and there is no stopping where you can go.

Many cyclists prefer to get their bike ride in early in the day, sometimes before the working day has even begun. Not only will it truly bring you round from the lethargy of sleep, it can invigorate you for the day. Research has even shown that morning exercise increases daily productivity and could even contribute to a more successful career. A 2011 survey of more than 2000 people found that 63 per cent of those who exercised in the morning (twice a week) believed exercise made them more effective at work. And the higher proportion of those earning above the national average were those we exercised before they started their day jobs.

A lack of energy could be another sign that you are struggling to get through the day. A fitter body will have much bigger energy levels and rather than wanting to nap on the sofa come early evening, a body and mind full of energy will go out and live, and pack their days full to the brim.

It's good to get outside

Those who have experienced mental health issues, specifically depression, have a tendency to sometimes stay indoors, away from not only people, but also the outside world itself.

Sunshine can massively help improve mood, self-esteem and outlook on life. In some extreme cases, light therapy can be prescribed to people, as research has shown it can aid with depression.

But there's nothing like the real thing. An hour ride in the sunshine, with the wind flying through your hair and the world passing by will really help. The sunlight can also have positive physiological effects.

Vitamin D is very important, as the minerals are vital for healthy bones. A lack of vitamin D can also lead to rickets and osteomalacia, which causes bone pain and tenderness.

Our body creates most of our vitamin D from exposure of direct sunlight onto our skin. And while we can attain vitamin D from parts of our diet, the sun is the best source.

Ask an expert

Helen Carter

How exercise can help depression

As a coach for over 20 years, Helen brings an expertise in the body (with a PhD in exercise physiology), the mind (from her study of Western psychology and Eastern philosophy), and relational dialogue (from her training in humanistic psychotherapy). Through her service 'Mind Body Dialogue', she helps people create a vision of how they want their life to be and facilitates moving them towards the desired outcome.

For more details visit www.mindbodydialogue.com.

'One in 10 Europeans have reportedly suffered from depression giving rise to its label as 'the disease of the century'. More research studies are coming on line supporting regular physical activity in both the reduction and prevention of depression. There is a need to counter the ever-increasing speed of our lives. To understand how exercise ameliorates depression we need to understand the four key players in the chemistry of mood state. First we have serotonin, a neurotransmitter that serves to elevate mood, increase feelings of satiety, and lift depression. Next there is dopamine, which in the main is responsible for sleeping and waking cycles. Then come two chemicals perhaps more familiar to athletes, the hormones adrenalin (responsible for getting our body to act) and endorphin (the body's 'natural painkiller'). All four are suppressed with chronic stress and anxiety, but also with society's common strategies of numbing distress e.g. alcohol, coffee intake.

Exercise can help return these bodily chemicals back towards normal levels. Low to moderate exercise that can be sustained for longer periods of time is best: high intensity work does kick start the adrenalin response, but this can interfere with sleep and also negatively impact on dopamine. It is worth remembering that these chemicals work in complex interaction with one another: it is best to experiment (with the help of a physical trainer or coach) to see which type of activity is best suited to your own unique physiology, diet and lifestyle.

Exercising outside in natural light can also bring a big boost to mood. It is commonly known that a lack of sun contributes to conditions such as Seasonal Affective Disorder in which hypothalamus function is impeded. This affects the production of the hormones melatonin and serotonin, thus distorting the body's circadian rhythm. Sunlight also underpins vitamin D metabolism, and a lack of this key nutrient is linked to depression. A final factor that cannot be overlooked is the benefit that comes from being with others. Increased social interaction can help depression sufferers to rebuild self-esteem, which in turn feeds in to maintaining and developing positive relationships and friendships.'

Structure and purpose

Many people who are experiencing depression and other mental health problems, struggle to find a lack of purpose or direction, which could be due to a number of reasons.

Sport stars for example are susceptible to depression once they have retired, due to the lack of structure in their lives. The same, in some cases, can be applied to the everyday person. Losing a job, a break up with a partner, or even coming to the end of something you have been involved in for a substantial amount of time, whether that's a professional or personal project. Of course there are many other triggers, but these are just a few that cause problems such as depression. Exercise creates a purpose. A reason to go out and do something.

Give yourself a goal

Set yourself something to do. Perhaps enter a sportive, a countryside all-day ride, a multi-day event, or even set a weight loss goal? Anything that gives you the chance to set out a plan, and allow you something to stick to.

Keep yourself busy. Bike riding gets you healthy, both physically and mentally.

Cycling goals help create structure and a sense of purpose in one's life. Set one now and start working to achieve it.

Get it written down. Print out a timetable and fill it. Fill it to the brim so that it's bursting out at the sides. When you look at it, it should feel daunting. That's good, it shows you're busy and there's not a spare minute in the day to be sitting on your backside.

Have your goal circled. Stick it on the fridge, on the kitchen cupboards or your bedside tables. Keep being reminded of it. It will act as motivation and a reminder that you have something to do.

Don't let one missed day become a week

Understandably, there will come days where you won't have the motivation and energy to get out and ride. And there is no shame in that. We're not here to shout and scream and tell you to get out of bed and ride your bike.

But don't let the day off turn into two days off. Because before you know it, a week would've passed and you haven't lifted a finger. You'll find yourself stuck in rut, your fitness levels would've taken a backward step and you'll be starting from square one again.

Now you may be reading this thinking who are we and what do we know about mental health problems. And you're right; we're no experts in this field.

But we do know the huge positive impacts cycling can have on the physiological and psychological aspects of the mind body.

We do know that exercise such as cycling can create friendships, create a reason to get out into the outside world, force you to make the effort, get you healthy, push you out into the sunshine and forge a reason for being.

Ask an expert
Helen Carter

Setting realistic goals

Helen Carter suggests that the way to achieving your goals through sport – and in particular through cycling – is to be realistic about what is possible.

'From an early age we are introduced to structure and routine – for example going to school and receiving a timetable to adhere to. Humans, on the whole, function very well with certainty. Routines help shape our days and give us purpose: something to get us up in the morning and to orientate our days. These routines ensure we have progression, whether it is getting an education, building a career or starting a family: all these projects lend a feeling of moving toward something and making the most of our lives. We are achieving things and are contributing to a bigger picture.

Then, we hit a life transition (the cliché mid-life crisis for example) and commonly, we question our life purpose. We have ticked all the boxes: the career, the family. 'What now?' Holes begin to appear and we question, 'What's the point?' Depression around the meaning of life has become more significant with more people choosing to live outside the frameworks offered by religion or faith systems. Many writers on depression and life purpose agree however: that we are solely responsible for creating meaning in our life. Setting goals is a great way to bring shape and drive back to our lives.

Sport remains a very accessible and fairly straightforward goal-driven project. This is evidenced by the popularity of middle-aged people coming back in to sport after establishing a career and family. Sporting goals can be particularly rewarding if allied to charitable causes. Satisfaction and life meaning are greatly enhanced when we help others. The key to success is to set realistic goals and use them to stretch us, not to push us. There is a fine line between settings goals that bring joy in mastering an activity and those that end up 'mastering us'! The serial setting of goals as a substitute of self-esteem needs to be cautioned against, and why working with a coach is advisable.'

Mindfulness

11

Practising mindfulness

In our busy lives we are often thinking about what we have done and what we are going to do next; seldom do we actually live in the right now. Learning to be in the moment is good for our health and our happiness.

In the rush of everyday life even as we are doing one task we are often thinking about the next one we need to do, but we only ever have the moment we are in. If we pass through it unaware we are missing an opportunity for experience, we lose touch with ourselves and the world we are living in. Mindfulness means paying attention in a particular way: on purpose, in the present moment and non-judgementally. This kind of attention increases awareness, clarity and acceptance. Being mindful is the opposite of taking life for granted. Many people think that the route to mindfulness is meditation but you can experience it in everyday life just by fully engaging all of your senses on the moment you are in, observing and feeling what is going on inside your body and in the environment around you.

Being a bike rider helps us to be more mindful without necessarily even realising we are doing it. If you are planning a ride you might well step outside your door to see what the weather is doing. Does the sky look like it might rain? How warm is it? Which direction is the wind blowing? These are all useful things that will help you plan what to wear and where to ride but also brings you closer to the natural world and engages your senses. The rider who doesn't do these things may well find themselves 10 miles from home, soaking wet without a jacket and slogging into a head wind!

Free your mind

The simple, repetitive action of cycling does not require constant thought so it can liberate your mind allowing you to be aware of your body and all the sensations of the environment you are passing through. Listening to your body is a useful exercise in knowing how hard you are cycling and how your body is responding, Be aware of the sensations in your muscles and your joints, where is there tension, do you feel any discomfort? The depth and frequency of your breathing will tell

you a lot about how much effort you are putting in and how comfortable you are with that effort. This is useful if you are using cycling to improve your fitness – see pages 138–39 – but if you are just out for a ride it may also help you to discover something about your emotional state.

We often carry our moods and emotions into the way we move and pedal our bikes so this can help you identify how you are actually feeling in that moment. You might not have realised how much pent-up aggression you had felt in a difficult business situation earlier in the day as you kept your cool and managed it professionally but getting on your bike may unleash those feelings and you can spot them in the way you are riding. Are you dawdling along in a daydream or hammering hard to expel some anger or get away from something unpleasant? Are you relaxed and breathing deeply or are your shoulders tense and you are breathing rapidly from your chest? You don't need to do anything to control or change how you are riding just be observant to it.

Familiarity breeds distraction

If you ride to work at the same time every day, on the same route and it takes the same amount of time there is a likelihood that you will turn up at the office and have very little memory of what actually happened on your ride as you would have been so wrapped up in planning the day ahead. Unless something extraordinary happens to shock us into being 'in the moment' it is very easy to drift through an often-repeated journey without being really alive to it.

Next time you are out on your favourite ride or on your commute to work try actively engaging your senses with the experience you are having. Work through them all in turn, be aware of your body on the bike and the feel of turning the pedals, feel the texture of the air as it passes over your skin and listen to the noise of the wind in your ears to help gauge how fast you are going.

Listen to the birds (and everything else)

If you listen you will hear (and experience) all kinds of things from birdsong to traffic noise, the music coming from a car radio, a lawnmower behind a garden wall, a rustle of leaves and even, on a really still day or in a quiet environment, the buzz and chirp of insects in the grass. Being on your bike instead of in a car means not only can you hear what is around you but you can smell it too; the smells of the countryside are often more obvious whether it is damp hedgerows, flowers or the stench of cow manure but even in an urban environment there are wafts of food cooking or the open door of a pub. Even if it is a route you are really familiar with taking time to look around you can reveal new things just by looking for them instead of drifting through.

Safety and awareness

We know a lot of people like to listen to music while they ride but be aware that if your music is up loud you are blocking off one of your senses. Being able to hear traffic around you can warn you of what is taking place behind you. On a quiet road the sound of car in the distance will prepare you for it over taking you, in an urban environment fast gear changes and revving might alert you to a driver about to come past in a dangerous or aggressive way. At junctions listening for traffic is as important as looking for it. Make sure your music is at a level that still lets the background noise permeate.

Breathing

Breathing isn't something we think about very often. If we had to think about every breath we would barely have time for anything else! However how you breath can have a profound effect on you're health and well being as well as how you feel while cycling.

How you breathe whether on the bike or in everyday life can affect your posture, your energy and stress levels. Shallow, fast breaths taken from the top of the lungs can increase tension in your shoulders leading to muscular discomfort and can also signal to your body that there is a problem. Adrenaline levels increase and your body reacts as if preparing for fight or flight. If you take fewer breaths, but make them deeper you get more oxygen with less effort. Breathing deeply accesses the lower lobes of the lungs where the exchange of gases is greatest, thus increasing breathing efficiency. It also relieves the strain on the muscles around your neck and shoulders which will be working more than they should be if your breathing is fast and high up in your lungs.

While you are cycling your breathing rate can give you lots of information about your fitness and how hard you are trying. It can tell you if you are taking it easy or if you are

trying hard. When you first start cycling, especially if you haven't done much exercise for a while, you may find your breath becoming short and rapid, it may even feel like you are struggling to catch your breath. Learning to slow down your breathing will help you feel stronger and more in control as well as helping you to gauge your effort more effectively.

When you begin cycling, the best pace for building your fitness is one that you can still comfortably talk at. As you progress and if you want to start improving your fitness by introducing some more structured training into your rides, monitoring your breathing is the first step of determining training zones. Observing your breathing can be just as effective as using a heart rate monitor to make sure you are exercising at the right level. Experienced cyclists even use their breathing to maintain a consistent pedal rate of around 90 rpm or revolutions per minute by synchronising pedal cadence and breath. See the box below to find out how you can monitor your breathing to make sure you are working at the right effort level to improve your fitness.

Breathing apparatus

Your diaphragm is a large muscle that fills the lower part of your chest cavity and abdomen. It is designed to move constantly with little fatigue. You will need a lot less energy to breathe if you are primarily using this dome-shaped muscle custom built for the task than the delicate secondary respiratory muscles around the neck, upper back and upper chest. Unfortunately the cycling position does not help us to access the lower part of the lungs, the hunched-over position means the abdomen is compressed and the diaphragm is less able to expand.

Before practising deep breathing on the bike try you need to learn how it feels off the bike. Lie on the floor and place one hand on your belly and one hand on your sternum. Start by just observing your breath, if your top hand is moving more you are breathing high up and shallowly just into the top part of your lungs. Begin to slow your breathing down directing the air you breathe down toward your belly. See if you can get your top hand to stay still so just the hand on your abdomen is moving.

It is much harder to do this when cycling but you can start by practising it when riding at a comfortable easy pace. Deliberately suck air deep into your lungs and feeling your sides, back and stomach expand. As your pace increases your breathing rate is likely to increase and creep back up to the top of your lungs, tune into it and see if you can slow it down again. This is a particularly useful technique when on a long climb as it both calms you and helps with your pace setting by giving you something to focus on.

Breathing to release stress

If you are under pressure at work and are becoming increasingly tense pause for a moment and observe your breath. Trying to breathe deeply will calm your parasympathetic nervous system, get more oxygen to your brain and help bring your stress levels down. While cycling taking deeper breaths at a slower rate will use a greater percentage of your lungs as well as helping to get more oxygen to your hardworking legs.

Improving observation

Some would think that cycling, if anything, would make you less observant. After all, it's ever so easy to switch into autopilot when out in the lanes and cycle by without a thought passing through your mind.

But in actual fact, your mind is constantly working when you're out riding and it can massively help your observation when you're off the bike, as well as your reaction times and your general awareness.

You may not think it, but adjusting your weight on the bike due to strong wind conditions, adding or taking off layers when the temperature rises or drops, shifting gears when approaching a climb or flying down an ascent, changing lines due to road debris or potholes, coming in at the right angle on a bend, and of course, awareness of other cars, cyclists and traffic lights are all actions made consciously by your mind.

So without necessarily realising, your mind is constantly working and making decisions.

Research has also shown that cycling can actually boost brainpower. Researchers from Illinois University found that a five per cent improvement in cardio respiratory fitness from cycling led to an improvement of up to 15 per cent in mental tests.

According to the researchers, this is due to exercise being able to help build new brain cells in the hippocampus, which is the region responsible for memory.

This isn't the only study to look at exercise and the positive relationship it has on brainpower.

A significant study from Hamburg, Germany had more than 60 men take part in a cycling programme over the course of several days. The control group did no exercise. At the end of the programme both groups had to complete a memory test. The results showed that the active group did better on the memory and recognition tests and believed that the improvement was down the exercise they had done.

Taking cycling into other areas of your life

Riding your bike through quiet lanes or busy city streets not only increases your awareness when you're on the bike, but also when you're off it.

If you happen to be a car driver as well, you'll realise just how exposed cyclists are and your tolerance and appreciation of other road users will increase.

There are certain groups that believe every car driver should take a cycling efficiency test. Is this a good idea? Quite possibly.

We have already shown that exercise can increase brainpower and productivity, but there are other areas that it can help as well.

Formula 1 driver Mark Webber is a very keen cyclist and he feels the cycling has helped increase his reactions when driving.

England cricketer, Matt Prior is another sportsman who has taken to two wheels. Not only has it helped him build up a weakened Achilles tendon, it has also improved his fitness, strength and co-ordination.

Remember that a more observant brain is one that reacts quicker, makes better decisions and is awake to its surroundings. Cycling may help your brain to function better.

Challenge yourself

12

Old dog, new tricks

The mental health charity MIND reports that there are five things we can do as we age to keep ourselves healthy. These are: to connect with others, be active, take notice of the world around us, keep learning and give help to others. Cycling ticks a lot of these boxes but in this chapter we are going to look at how cycling can be a way to learn new skills and how that can improve the health of your brain.

Just as cycling helps to keep our bodies in good working order, so can exercising our brains help us to stay mentally agile. Even as we age we can continue to grow new connections among the billions of brain cells we possess by learning new things, while daily brain challenges may help to ward off dementia. The newness of a skill is important because as you become competent at a task the less challenging it is to the training brain. Taxing the brain by learning new tasks is vital to long-term brain health.

As well as exercising your brain intellectually it also needs physical activity to maintain the cardiovascular flow. Our brains have the most blood vessels of any of our organs. So the combination of learning new cycling skills and being physically active gives your brain a double boost.

Learning new skills is deeply satisfying: if you've looked on with envy at the cyclists track-standing at lights or nonchalantly riding along no-handed then it may be time to challenge yourself to learn something new.

Ride like a child

Building skills on a bike as an adult is harder than when you are a child: we have a much stronger sense of self-preservation so are far less likely to take physical risk. If you haven't done much sport or physical activity since childhood you may also have lost confidence in your ability to do certain things.

When children start cycling they are excited to try new things, prepared to push their boundaries and take a few risks. The desire to accomplish something new is very high in kids. As adults we have already encountered 'failing' at things so are more afraid to have a go. Children aren't really conscious of what other people think of them but as adults we are afraid of looking silly, not being able to do something well or simply acting in way we think may be isn't appropriate.

So how can we drop this fearful mind-

Ways to play

Practise weaving in out of obstacles on the ground. Find small markers and place them at first two bike lengths apart. Use your body to steer the bike instead of making sharp turns with the handlebars. Increase your speed and gradually put the markers closer and closer together.

Just one hand
Get used to riding with only one hand on the bars by reaching down for your water bottle, getting things out of your back pocket or simply practise touching different parts of your bike.

Move closer
Move your hand to the top tube, down tube, behind your saddle. If you ride with other people, practise getting closer together, so you can ride side by side and gently bump hands or hips. Try placing a hand on your friend's shoulder or even try holding hands, as it will help you to get closer to each other.

Stop in time
Practise accurate braking by putting a marker down and riding towards it aiming to stop with your front wheel dead level. See how moving your body weight changes the way your bike stops. See how fast you can go and still stop accurately but remember to be careful of that powerful front brake.

set and learn to 'play' on our bikes and why should we? Becoming a more skilful rider will make you more confident, more in control and often you will find more fun in your bike as you will be able to swoop through corners and enjoy the sensations of speed. Practising skills in a safe environment will mean they become second nature to you so if something does happen say when riding in traffic or on a downhill you'll be able to quickly and safely respond.

New skills should be practised in a fun, safe environment where the consequences of taking risks are low. This could be a park, a quiet road or even your own driveway. Having the support of other riders around you can encourage you to push yourself and try new things.

There are many beginner-coaching sessions around the country where adult cyclists can practise skills in a fun but supportive way. Bikeability run courses for adult cyclists as well as children, you can find out more at www.dft.gov.uk. They offer group and one to one courses and will also be able to help you with planning and safely riding routes in your local area. Just remember when it comes to playing around on a bike if you are laughing, you are learning, even if as a sensible, mature adult you think you are 'wasting time' mucking about, the skills you develop will prove invaluable out on the road.

Key skills

Safe braking: Your bike has a front brake and a back brake: in the UK we use the left hand lever to operate the back brake and the right hand lever to operate the front brake. It is really important that you check which lever controls which brake before you start riding. The front brake is considerably more powerful as it has all the weight of you and your bike behind it, when you brake use your back brake, left hand, fractionally before your front brake to slow your bike down with control.

Confident cornering: When approaching a corner, make sure you brake while you are still in a straight line so that you are at the right speed when you enter the corner. Look for the exit as this will help put your body into the right position and help you steer a smooth line

through. Make sure your inside leg is up and your outside leg is down, push some weight through the straight outside leg as this will help your tyres grip. As soon as you are out the corner put in a couple of pedal strokes to get back up to speed.

Smooth descending: As with cornering the key to smooth descending is looking far enough ahead and measuring your speed appropriately. Keep your weight low and cover your brakes but avoid 'dragging' them, keeping them partially on all the way down the hill. Only use them when you need them to control your speed. Think about your leg position: in a straight line you may want your pedals level so you can evenly balance your weight on the bike and use your bent knees to absorb some of the jarring from the road. When rounding a corner you need to have your inside leg up and outside leg down as explained above.

Capable climbing: Climbing effectively has a lot to do with gear selection and pacing. When you see a hill ahead, change down into an easier gear before the gradient steepens otherwise it is hard to shift smoothly. Don't go straight to your easiest gear, as you need somewhere to go to if the hills become harder or you start to struggle. Aim to keep pedalling at around 60rpm, changing gear to maintain a comfortable effort level. Keep your head up and shoulders relaxed and breathe deeply into the bottom of your lungs, trying to keep your torso as still as possible when you are in the saddle. You may need to get out of the saddle and use your body weight to help add extra leverage to each pedal stroke if the hill is particularly steep.

One-hand: Riding with only one hand on the bars is absolutely essential to being safe on the road as you will need to be able to indicate left and right turns. First, move the hand that is going to remain on the bars nearer to the stem at the centre, if you are nervous start by taking off the other hand but holding it down to your side, once you become comfortable still riding in a straight line practise holding it out at right angles to your body. Practise with both hands.

No-hands: Smooth movements and confidence is key to riding without your hands on the bars, the main thing to remember is that if you feel wobbly you can simply go back to the tops so don't panic. Sit upright and central whilst keeping your shoulders relaxed as this will allow you to maintain balance and don't try to over-steer with your body. Look forward and up the road ahead rather than down at the bars.

Cycling is a fantastic sport for all shapes, sizes and ages and it's never too late to get started. There was a lean, mean, Lycra-clad man putting all the youngsters to shame on the hills at a recent trip to Majorca and when we stopped for coffee he revealed he was 83 and just getting serious about his riding.

One of the great things with cycling is that you'll find a really broad ranges of ages all riding and getting along together and perceptions of age go out the window. With a helmet and glasses on you never can tell the age of a fit cyclist and you can let your legs do the talking! Never think you're too old to achieve new things on a bicycle and whether you're starting as a teenager or much later in life there is a world of joy to be discovered on two wheels.

Geroldine Glowinski took part in her first road race at the age of 40. Now at 54 she's loving her bike more than ever. The part-time bookkeeper for an engineering company, occasional property developer and main carer for her 85-year-old mum explains why cycling keeps her so happy and why it's never too late to get started.

'I took up cycling at the age of 38, never having ridden before. All my family cycled, so I'd support them and fetch and carry but then I saw an advert from The Anerley Cycle Club volunteering to take out beginner women and that was it – I was hooked!

'At first I just wanted to do social rides, then longer rides and harder rides were on offer. It was suggested I do time trials, a race against the clock. Then, at the age of 40, I did my first road race and loved the adrenaline rush.

'Depending on the season, I usually do a long ride of 70-85 miles on a Tuesday (my day off) with a group called 'Over the Hill Gang' around Surrey, Sussex and Kent. Then on a

Sunday I'll do a club ride with Velo Club Londres (VCL) who are a fantastic family club based at Herne Hill Velodrome, that's usually 30-40 miles.

I do a 'fast' ride – either sprint training by myself for about an hour and a half or a 'derny' session at the track (behind a big motor bike which gets faster and faster) and I do an occasional road race or track race. I never dreamt I'd be doing this sort of riding but I love it! In the summer I do regular sportives and winter MTB rides. I'm definitely a 'jack of all trades and master of none'.

'Cycling has such a good feel factor; when I've finished doing an event I like the feeling of really having pushed myself and even the feeling of being totally wrecked is good.

'Independent is another word that springs to mind, to go off for a few hours being aware of the seasons and nature – what could be better?

'Winning the SCCU 100 Women's time trial a few years ago and road racing in a small town in France at nearly 40 degrees have to be two of my proudest moments. I was pipped at the post and came second, but the French locals made me feel like a champion although I do think they got a shock when I took of my helmet and sunglasses and they saw my 'advanced' years.

'Cycling is the most social of sports to mix with people of all genders, ages and social backgrounds. I often don't know what the person I'm riding with does in 'real' life, but it doesn't matter as we have cycling in common and we have to often rely on one another. My cycling friends involve me in theatre, walking, partying and holidays.

'Regarding health – cycling has given me stamina and confidence. I am rarely ill and can eat what I like. I would say to other riders, 'don't waste time, just get on and do it.' I was terribly nervous at first and I took a long time to get used to anything new for example, cleats and pedals. So if I can do it anyone can. It will bring you many great memories and life is about memories. And there is no better beauty regime than being happy and cycling makes me happy.'

case study *Rediscoving a former passion*

Ivor Bennett, 54, started participating in road racing and time trials when he was 13 and admits he gave it up at the age of 17 when girls came on the scene.

Proving it's never too late to get back into cycling he started mountain biking in October 2010 at the age of 51 and has never felt better. 'I didn't intend to get back into it to be honest. I asked my brother about bikes, as I wanted to buy one just to cycle to the pool, because at the time I was swimming regularly. Needless to say since I bought the bike I haven't been swimming!

'I'm shattered after a three-hour ride on the trails nearby, but I love it! Very rarely am I at the front of the pack on a Monday or Thursday night ride, and on occasions the group have to wait for me to get my breath back, but still really enjoy pushing myself hard, regardless of not being in my twenties!

'What does cycling mean to me? Pain! Seriously though, it's about keeping fit, and it's such a great way to socialise with good mates while enjoying the outdoors, whatever the weather.

'There are so many health benefits. Since I started cycling again I definitely feel better in myself. I've lost weight although I still have a few kg to lose. Despite a few setbacks and the fact that my knees and legs take a while to recover after a hard ride it's all worth it.

'My favourite moments on the bike include mountain biking on quality single track, ideally downhill, fast!'

Health and immunity

13

Exercise and longevity

Without wanting to state the blindingly obvious, those who exercise regularly and eat a balanced diet are much healthier and fitter than those who don't.

But what are the reasons for this? Well, there isn't one straight answer to this question. In fact, there are several factors, and the good news is, there are even more benefits to be had from cycling.

Weight loss: Cycling is a great way to burn excess calories, lose unwanted pounds and improve general health. A single one-hour ride can burn anything up to 400 calories, depending on your body weight. Many cyclists adhere to the fat burning zone, which is commonly misinterpreted as the best exercise intensity for losing weight. While it's correct that at lower intensity, the body predominantly burns fat as this provides the largest fuel resource for the muscle, this isn't where you will lose more weight. Quite simply, you won't lose weight if you aren't working your muscles hard enough. If you want to lose weight, you will need to work hard, and the harder you work, the more calories you will burn.

Healthy heart: When regarding the heart and its health, quite simply, the bigger the better (so as long as all the heart's chambers are in proportion). Cyclists have larger hearts than most people. Cardiovascular exercise such as cycling increases the size of the heart's chamber and the thickness of the muscular walls that contract to pump blood around the body. An increased volume of blood pumped is able to pump around the body with each beat, which in turn results in the heart needing to beat fewer times per minute at rest than an untrained one. Not only that, but oxygenated blood will be able to get to your working muscles much quicker and bring back oxygen-depleted blood at a faster rate. This means that those with a larger heart will be able to exercise harder and for longer.

Sleep is an important part of health: A lack of sleep will not only cause physical fatigue but mental tiredness as well. It can also cause grumpiness, make you short tempered and have a negative effect on decision-making and concentration. There have even been some studies to suggest that a lack of sleep can contribute to weight gain. And while there is a lot of advice out there from health experts or internet forums to help make your way to the land of nod that little easier, there's no better substitute than exercise. Results from a number of studies have shown that exercise leads to improved sleep quality, longer sleep and the ability to fall asleep more quickly. However, don't exercise too late in the day. The National Sleep Foundation recommends avoiding heavy exercise so close to bed time, as physical exertion and sweating has been shown to have an adverse effect on sleep quality.

Bigger and more toned thighs: Casting aside the fact that a larger leg with more muscle is able to produce more power and push the bike further and faster, one would imagine the only other benefit of a toned leg is that of vanity. However, there's more to it than that, and a pair of large, shapely pins may be more beneficial than you think. In a study published in the British Medical Journal, researchers found a significant positive link between thigh size and the risk of heart disease and premature death.

According to the study, there may be a link between those with smaller thighs and a higher risk of heart disease because they indicate a lower than normal muscle mass in that region, which could be a factor in triggering the development of type two diabetes, and in turn, heart disease. The great thing with cycling is, the more you do of it, the larger your legs will become.

case study Getting fit again

Cycling is one of the quickest ways back to overall fitness and a healthy lifestyle no matter what your starting point, as **Scott Wells**, 28, explains.

'The thought of getting up at 7am and riding 10 miles to work in the morning is something that I never thought I could even do, let alone actually end up enjoying. But 12 months ago I decided that after looking in the mirror every morning and not being happy with the body that was looking back at me I needed to do something about it and most importantly, stick to it. I had tried gyms but could never stick at it, mainly due to how repetitive it quickly become. It was only when a friend of mine who is a keen cyclist recommended that I invested in a road bike and start cycling to work. The idea sounded good and it just so happened that my employer is part of the governments cycle to work scheme. So I went ahead and purchased my first road bike and off I went.

I have to admit that in the first month or so it was hard work cycling to and from work but, as the pounds started to quickly drop and as my waistline got smaller, it become a lot easier and I was starting to enjoy getting up in the morning to cycle to work. It really is a breath of fresh air to be out on the road in the morning and enjoying the scenery on the way rather than staring at the same four walls in a packed and sweaty gym. The most important part of my journey is the fact that my health has vastly improved and I feel fitter and stronger then I ever have. Looking back I should have done this years ago.'

Even if you cycle all the time like **Matt Moran**, 36, it is worth taking a little time to think about what it really means to you.

'If I had to list all of the reasons why I like riding my bike then I probably wouldn't list 'helps me to stay fit' as one of them. But therein lies the beauty of cycling, I get to see some of the finest scenery on offer up close, smell the fresh air of the countryside after being tied to a desk all week and feel that child-like freedom as I hurtle down a hill on a bike. And all of this is helping me to stay healthy without me having to think about it. The daily reminders of being healthy or staying fit are all but lost to cyclists. Fitness is a wonderful by-product of the things that make cycling so great.

For me, there's no better way to clear the mind than a couple of hours on the bike, I'm sure some would need a week lying on a beach to achieve the same effect. Now and again I will train for a specific event, taking every pedal stroke seriously and then I'll spend the rest of the year just riding a bike for fun. Either way there'll always be somebody faster and slower than me on a bike.'

Live for longer: While it's common sense that the healthier one is, the more likely they are to live for longer, there is actual solid evidence to support this. A famous – in certain circles – Harvard Alumni study, examined mortality rates over a 22 to 26 year period in over 17,000 men. Results showed that those who expended 2000 calories per week during exercise lived on average, two years longer than those who did no exercise at all. What's even more staggering, was that the lead researcher, Ralph Paffenbarger, M.D., was able to work out a formula that summarised his results: for each hour that a person exercises, he or she gets roughly two extra hours of life! We're not too sure if that's a promising statistic or a downright frightening one.

Immunity: People will try almost anything to avoid getting ill: an apple a day, orange after orange, antiseptic wipes, hand gel – anything to keep unwanted bugs at bay. However, a lot of people ignore exercise, but it really does help build up a stronger immune system. While it's correct that exercise initially actually weakens the immune system, over a period of time, regular activity has shown a positive immune system response and a boost in the production of macrophages (the cells that attack bacteria).

Sex: Now that got your attention and so it should. Cycling will improve your sex life. A healthier body, larger heart, increased cardiovascular fitness, stronger thighs and buttocks, all will make life in the sack that little bit more fun, and last that little bit longer.

Pollution and health

By now you should be aware of why cycling is the greatest sport in the world. OK, that might be pushing it a little, but there's no denying that cycling can do wonders for the body and the mind. The evidence, research and first hand stories from cyclists themselves does enough to prove that.

However, it's not all plain sailing and there are certain issues that you must be aware of. It wouldn't be fair on the sport of cycling unless we painted the whole picture.

One of the biggest issues is that of pollution and the impact it has on the respiratory system. And with more people commuting to work, bike hire schemes and people taking up riding in general, air pollution is a real problem.

We don't want to put people off cycling through the city – the more individuals that ride, the less cars there will be on the roads – but many are unaware about the potential damage that air pollution could be doing to their lungs.

What is air pollution?

Air pollution is a number of pollutants in the air that have certain effects on the lungs. Pollution from diesel engines for example is a major concern for cyclists. These particulates from diesel engines are extremely small and can be inhaled further down into the lungs whereas larger particles can't. These can cause significant airway irritation and breathing problems, especially for those who already have existing respiratory disease.

The effects of air pollution

Air pollution can have a number of effects on the body, most notably the lungs. Primarily, they cause the airways to become inflamed. As the airways increase in size, they narrow, which can cause irritation and decrease the amount of oxygen that the blood can carry. This inevitably has a negative effect on the functioning of the lungs.

Cyclists are in a vulnerable position on the roads. Riding behind cars, trucks, mopeds; all vehicles that splutter out harmful gases. It doesn't help that cycling puts a lot of stress on the respiratory system, causing the lungs to dig deep for air to get oxygen to the working parts of the body. So not only are cyclists more exposed to potentially harmful gases, they are breathing in much deeper – some studies have indicated that cyclists can inhale up to five times more particulates than either car users and those travelling on public transport.

However, there have been some studies, which seem to suggest the opposite, and it is actually the passengers travelling by foot, cars or buses that are at most risk. The reason being that they are 'stuck' in an environment of limited circulating ventilation, whereas the cyclist is able ride away from polluted areas.

A 2004 study published in the Health Promotion Journal of Australia found that motorists registered the highest levels for all pollutants, 'while cycling commuters had significantly lower levels of exposure compared with car users.'

Dealing with pollution

• Car fumes quickly dissipate, so riding upright will limit the effect of the fumes.

• Although it's not always possible due to your own work schedule, try and ride before or after peak hours, as there will be fewer vehicles on the road.

• Try and keep your distance from exhaust pipes.

• Move out in front of vehicles when stopped at lights.

Cycling and diabetes

Figures released in 2013 revealed that around three million people are thought to have diabetes across the country with an estimated 850,000 who have undiagnosed Type 2 diabetes. Cycling can help to burn off excess glucose so can help people manage diabetes and for many Type 2 diabetes sufferers the condition can be controlled with good diet and exercise so riding brings a lot of benefits.

Pav Kalsi, a clinical advisor at Diabetes UK explains: 'There is good evidence to show that if you identify 'pre-diabetes' in the early phases, prevention is possible. A physical activity of moderate intensity, such as cycling could be a good way to do this.'

If you already have Type 1 or Type 2 diabetes cycling can help to prevent further complications, meaning you can live a perfectly normal life, keeping your weight in check and contributing to a healthy lifestyle.

Foot focus

According to Diabetes UK, 'Foot problems can affect anyone who has diabetes, whether they are being treated with insulin, tablets, non-insulin injections or diet and physical activity only.

'People with diabetes are more likely to be admitted to hospital with a foot ulcer than with any other complication of diabetes. This is because diabetes may lead to poor circulation and reduced feeling in the feet.'

For this reason, good footwear is an important factor during cycling for diabetes sufferers and if you notice any colour changes, blisters or swelling you must give it attention straight away and seek medical advice.

case study How cycling helps my diabetes

Andrew French, 42, was diagnosed with Type 1 diabetes in 2003 and explains why he won't let it hold him back.

'I compete at a good standard of amateur cycle racing and this really does help to allow me to have excellent blood sugar control. Mixing a full time job, a young family and cycling is difficult but the benefits of all the training pay off in blood sugar control. I ride about 10 hours or more a week.

'I have to plan my day to a sensible structure. From the moment I get up I check my blood, ensure I take my background insulin shot – I have a dual insulin regime, slow acting insulin once a day and fast acting with food – and then depending on what I am doing manage my levels accordingly. I would stress it's not something that's onerous, rather just part of my life and I certainly don't let diabetes control my life it's just part of it.

'Having raced to a good standard before being diagnosed with Type 1 diabetes and also after diagnosis the only change is to make sure that I start a ride with levels slightly higher than normal to ensure I can get round the route plus an energy gel or two, but I carried these before my condition too.

'Certainly cycling has been a huge help providing a much flatter blood sugar profile and obviously it is great for general fitness, allowing me to easily maintain a healthy weight as well as keeping me sane.'

'The biggest challenge is hot weather and exercise as I find my levels drop much more quickly in hotter weather especially when I am training.

'I have cycled and competed for years now, I don't race anymore as family life means I try to spend as much time as I can with my boys and wife but I still train every day on the bike or in the gym or just go for an hour long run.

'There are no foods I don't eat, simply a mantra of everything in moderation and having a balanced diet

'Cycling means a huge amount to me, I love riding and have always been sporty which I can now share with my boys, who both like riding with Daddy.'

Bounce back

14

Cycling and resilience

Resilience is a necessary skill for coping with stress and adversity, it's a way to describe how we can bounce back from difficult life events, and bend, not break, when we are under pressure. If we are resilient we can gain strength and even experience personal growth from the way we deal with difficulties, as the saying goes, 'what doesn't kill me makes me stronger'. Knowing that we have the skills to cope when things go wrong it also makes us more open to new experiences and more willing to take risks. Being resilient and able to find ways to get through and adapt in difficult circumstances is an important aspect of leading a happy and fulfilling life.

Resilience is not a character trait; it is something that can be developed. We can improve our ability to adapt to change and to gain the skills that will allow us to bounce back from adversity so that we are ready for whatever life throws at us. Facing some sort of adversity in our lives increases our resilience by enabling us to find ways of coping, engage with other people for support and to understand that our awareness and attitude towards situations influences our ability to bounce back from difficulty. If we are not prepared for adversity we may feel helpless or give up in the face of challenges.

But what you may be asking has this to do with cycling? Resilience is an important area of research for sports psychologists as athletes who show resilience are more likely to be successful and as well as more likely to have a long productive careers. Coaches and team psychologists will deliberately put riders into unexpected and difficult situations to see how they handle them. Over time, with analysis and self-awareness, athletes learn strategies to cope so that when things go wrong for real when in a race they handle the situation in way that is both practical but also doesn't affect their

mental state so that they can re-focus on the competition.

There are many aspects of sport that require resilience and the skills learnt from it are also highly transferable to other areas of your life. By putting yourself into difficult situations through cycling and sport you can start to build the skills and experience that will help you to bounce back from other tricky situations.

We rehearse how we will behave in a crisis in our everyday lives, if the worst happens to us we won't suddenly change our behaviour; we will fall back on what we are already doing. If our way of dealing with a failure on the bike, for instance struggling with a particularly steep hill, is to keep trying riding a little further each time before having to get off, then we will be more likely to keep working at other things in our areas of our lives, particularly because we will have learned that perseverance paid off. If we deal with a puncture by panicking about being stranded and calling for help immediately we are missing out on an opportunity to positively and calmly look for solutions and prove our own competency by fixing it.

Starting exercise proves to you that your body is a work in progress, as you ride more you'll see a difference in your legs, muscles will become firmer and more prominent, you may lose a bit of body fat, you'll be able to ride further and faster the more riding you do. A key belief in the study of resilience is that our intelligence can similarly be shaped. If we believe our intelligence to be fixed then it is hard to strive for further self-awareness, if we believe it to be malleable, a work in progress, then every situation, every success and failure is an opportunity for learning.

Cycle coaches will try and build resilience in their athletes by throwing in occasional difficult tasks that require them to go just a little bit further than they have been comfortable with before. For example your coach sets you off to do six maximal sprint efforts, at the end of it you feel exhausted and think you have given it your all, then he asks you for a seventh. By doing the seventh effort, even though you think you are exhausted, you are challenging your belief in what you can do and proving your resilience.

It is a common complaint at the end of organised rides that the organisers had 'thrown in an extra hill'. If you think you know how much you need to do you measure your efforts accordingly but if that extra hill does appear on your route you will be able to handle it, if you have the right mindset.

Ways to increase your resilience

Set achievable goals This could be as simple as completing a certain length of ride, riding to work every day for a month or conquering a tough hill without walking. Simply giving yourself a challenge to overcome will give you a sense of mastery.

Go out of your comfort zone Cycling is supposed to be fun but it does us all good to push our boundaries occasionally. You don't need to push them in a physical way, it could be the challenge of taking part in an event, or going on a group cycling holiday where you would be meeting people for the first time.

Teach yourself a new skill Learn to do something mechanical with your bike such as fix a puncture. This will give you confidence to ride alone but also developing competence, and particularly competence under stress, is a key skill in building resilience.

Setbacks are temporary A setback is just that, a step backwards on your path or an obstacle. In cycling a setback could be an injury or a week of missed rides due to a busy situation at work, but a setback is not permanent. This is a belief that can be applied to all areas of your life.

Recovering from illness and injury

At some point in your life, whether you like it or not, you're going to fall victim to an injury or illness. And there's nothing worse than building up a solid level of fitness, where you're happy with your weight, you're enjoying your riding, only for the rug to be pulled from under your feet.

Now hopefully the illness or injury will not be too serious, but either way, your fitness will take a backward step. Luckily, bike riding is a fantastic way to get back to full health, and perhaps come back even stronger.

How cycling helps recovery

Cycling is a non weight-bearing activity, which means it puts very little force through the joints of the body. This is perfect for those of you who have aching joints, suffer from arthritis, or simply experience discomfort when out exercising, as they won't be put under any further stress from cycling.

Many ex-footballers, rugby players, boxers – in fact athletes in a host of disciplines – take to cycling once their careers have finished, because it's an easy way to keep fit without breaking their already stressed bodies.

Similarly, those with larger frames may find it difficult to keep going when taking part in

weight bearing activities such as jogging, because their joints are carrying a heavier weight, and more force is exerted on them. With cycling, this isn't a problem. In fact, the only problem you may have is getting up the hills, but on the plus side, you will be able to dart down the other side.

The benefits of low-impact exercise

Many health advisors will advocate the use of a bicycle when returning from injury, because of its low impact nature and the very low likelihood of developing any further injuries. This means that you may be able to ride your bike while you are still 'injured' ensuring your fitness levels remain ticking over.

Cycling proved to be a real boon when tackling recurring and hard-to heal football – and other sports injuries as **Callum Tomsett**, 39, from West Sussex'explains.

'Having come from a background of football, I'm a relatively new starter to cycling. But I wished I had started earlier.

'As I started to get a bit older, my injuries became more frequent and they were taking longer to clear. There were times when I found myself completely unable to take part in any form of exercise. I'm not a member of the gym, and what with being a slightly bigger lad, I found it hard to go out for a run, as my joints would start to ache very quickly. In fact, running would often make my injuries worse.

'Cycling is perfect for me. It keeps me fit, it's something totally different to what I normally do, and it's put no excess force through my ankle, knees hips and back.

'I've found it's helped with my football, too. I'm much fitter, and am able to play for longer without tiring.

'When I now pick up an injury or strain, it doesn't mean I'm inactive for the next week. Instead, I will just give the football a miss go out on my bike and keep fit for when I return.

'In fact, what I'm now finding is, I'm riding more and playing less football. If someone told me that ten years ago I would've laughed them all the way out of the pub!'

Overcoming illness through cycling

Sometimes an illness can set you back further than an injury because it totally wipes out the body's defences, leaving you empty, unable to summon up the energy to do anything.

In this case, it's all about building your strength up through diet before you think about exercising. However, that's not to say a bike can't help and if you have space, an indoor bike is worth investing some money in.

Think about an exercise bike

Having an exercise tool within the comfort of your own home will increase the chances of you exercising, rather than having to wrap up and go for a run out in the elements. It's also more controlled. After a bout of illness, everything is off: your fitness, your motivation, your reactions and your concentration, so it's not wise to go out on the roads for a ride as accidents may happen. With a static bike, the uncontrollable factors are taken out of the equation, so you are able to 'switch off' and just ride.

Exercise actually helps defend against some illnesses. During moderate bouts of exercise, immune cells circulate through the body more quickly, enabling them to kill bacteria and viruses. Your body also releases endorphins when you exercise. Endorphins are known as the as natural pain relievers, and send the body into a state of a natural high once exercise has finished. Ever wondered what that buzz is you feel are a hard workout?

But you must be cautious when exercising so quickly after being ill. If you have had a fever, then refrain from cycling until it has fully cleared. It's extremely dangerous to exercise when the body still has a high temperature. Once this has gone down, and you feel healthy again, then it's safe to exercise.

The risk of osteoporosis

While the low impact nature of cycling is good for those who suffer from joint problems, osteoporosis or low bone mineral density is an issue that many cyclists face. In fact, research shows that cyclists have far more brittle bones in later life than those who partake in physical activity. To promote bone growth, the body needs impact to signal to the bones to create more mass. If you are only cycling, you will need exercises such as forms of weight training to increase strength and reduce the onset of osteoporosis.

case study *Coming back from illness*

Knowing how and when to use your bike when coming back from a bout of illness is the key, explains **Jo Beales**, 25, from Balham, south London.

'Getting sick is never nice. But the worst thing I find is not actually being ill, but the aftermath, once the virus has gone and you get that empty and weak feeling. It's as if you are starting from zero.

'I like to keep active whether that's cycling, running, playing golf, football, tennis, hockey you name it. But once an illness has subsided, it's very hard to get going again especially with ball sports such as hockey or tennis.

'That's what's so great about cycling. You're in control of what you want to do and how much you want to do. And if you have a static bike, it's even better. Being able to exercise in the comfort of your own home, not having to worry about a change in the weather, other cyclists or car drivers means you can concentrate on yourself and how you are feeling.

'You can also build yourself back up and physically see yourself getting fitter and stronger again.

'Don't get me wrong, I don't just use a bike as a form of rehabilitation, but it's certainly the best method that I have found to get active again and get my fitness levels back to where they should be.'

case study *Cycling through hard times*

Life can throw some unexpected events at you and coping isn't always easy. Cycling can play a part in helping to lift your mood and giving you something to focus on. Not only could you meet new people and make new friendships but getting out, exploring the great outdoors and pushing yourself physically can really take your mind off the negative experiences you are going through. A tough hill will allow you to focus on the burn in your legs as well as your breathing and the scenery and when you get to the top you'll feel a real emotional boost. Simply getting outdoors is the first step if you're grieving, going through a break-up or coping with stress and hopping on your bike can help you to do this.

When the going got tough for **Jo Fisken** she turned to her trusted friend, the bicycle.

'Cycling means so many things to me, it makes me feel free, makes me happy and gives me the space to think, going out with a group gives you a sense of belonging and riding alone can get you through that unforgiving minute.

'As for times of pressure, well my husband walked out on me and our children two years ago and without riding my bike I really don't think that I would have coped with the ups and downs. The group of people that I ride with keep me sane but it also gives me a vent for my anger and a reason to get up and out when I don't have the children. Having a bike to jump on at lunchtime at work has helped to give me escape from a busy day or to solve a problem. Once again riding my bike will help me through redundancy – I really could do with an uneventful year now – and the trials of job-hunting. The best thing about riding a bike is being able to escape, enjoy the countryside and feel great.

'I ride mountain bikes mainly but have in the last year have discovered the road bike which I love equally.

'As for memorable moments, there are so many from an amazing grin-inducing descent of Minch Moor Innerleithen, to getting my children riding single track for the first time, but our hike a bike tour of Skye has to be amongst the best yet, just for the amazingly huge views and the 'Did we really carry the bikes over that waterfall?' moment.

'Exercise definitely helps with stress; I don't know where I would be without my endorphin fix.'

15

Making friends

One of the joys of cycling is that it can be done in solitude, with one other person, a group of friends or even with thousands of others. Starting cycling can help to open up new social networks and connections, form new relationships and help you to feel part of a wider community of people with shared interests and passions.

Relationships with others are a key part of not just our happiness but also our health.

Research has shown that the quality and quantity of the relationships we have has a huge influence on our health and longevity, not just our emotional well-being. Not having close personal relationships has the same effect on our health as smoking or obesity. Being part of a network of social connections increases our immunity, lowers the risk of heart disease and reduces the decline in mental ability as we age. Being part of a large crowd of people with similar aims, such as in a cycling event like London to Brighton, can create feelings of camaraderie and even euphoria amongst participants.

So once you have a bike, how do you enter the wonderful community of cyclists? Well, a lot depends on your own personality type and how you want to engage with other people. Being part of a club or joining something isn't everyone's cup of tea but there are various ways you can take part in the community of cycling at a level you are comfortable with. You may have already noticed that simply riding a bike gives rise to casual social interaction as a bike gives you an excuse to chat when you meet a fellow cyclist at the train station or cafe. Even something as simple as a smile or a friendly nod to the rider coming the other way can brighten your day and make you feel a part of something. If you want to meet bike riders and become involved in events or rides it couldn't be easier.

Join the club

Cycling clubs have a long and historic history in the UK. There is a lot of debate over which is the oldest club in the UK but there are many clubs who have been continuously active from soon after the bicycle was invented in the late 1870s and early 1880s. Many of the older clubs had associations with the socialist movement or workers' rights and take a lot of pride in the history that they are a part of.

British Cycling has a club finder facility on its website: www.britishcycling.org.uk. This allows you to search by your own interests and find the clubs that offer beginners rides, coaching or women only sessions. Most clubs now have their own websites so you can get a sense of what to expect, however all clubs are different so it is worth asking around at your local bike shop as to which one will be the best for you. Some can be very serious with a strong sense of tradition and focus on racing; others are much more social and are simply about meeting up for group rides and encouraging newcomers.

Get out and ride

You don't have to join a club to take part in group rides or guided rides. British Cycling run Sky Rides that offer everything from big organised events to local rides with ride leaders who will guide the route and offer you tips and advice. You can find out more at www.goskyride.com. The Cyclists' Touring Club (CTC) is passionate about creating cycling

Make your own club

'I started Full Circle Cycles after a cycling holiday in Majorca; I loved riding with others and enjoyed the social element so much, I wanted to continue it back home. I found others were also riding by themselves but wanted to ride with others but not in a club environment. Full Circle Cyclists are a fun social network of cyclists. There are a mix of males and females and a mix of standards but the main aim is about having fun with coffee and cake being compulsory at the end of each ride!'

Jo Smith – founder of Full Circle Cycles

communities. They have members' groups all across the country that regularly organise led rides for all abilities (www.ctc.org.uk). Many of these events are free or require a small donation to cover costs; they are accessible to everyone and a great first experience of group riding.

Rides for women

Currently three times more men than women cycle for fun. Breeze is British Cycling's initiative to try and redress the balance. Breeze Champions are enthusiastic, knowledgeable female cyclists who take on the role of leading rides and offering support and advice. Rides normally start and end at cafés so you have a chance to chat with other riders. It doesn't matter how fast or slow, experienced or inexperienced you are these rides go at a pace to suit everyone. www.goskyride.com

Cycletta are entry-level sportive events just for women riders. Distances range between 20km and 80km so there is something for everyone. There are plenty of other sportive events that cover similar distances but if you like the idea of meeting other female cyclists and sharing your experiences or concerns these are fun events to get started with.

Events and sportives

Mass participation cycling events are growing rapidly in popularity. Wherever you are in the country you will be able to find something happening in your local area. The biggest UK

event is still London to Brighton in June every year; officially 20,000 riders take part but as many as double that join in for parts of the route.

Organised events, often called sportives, vary in length from 20km to 200km. Routes are sign-posted and offer feed stations and technical support along the way. They are timed but not competitive. You can challenge yourself to complete the route in a certain time to receive a gold, silver or bronze award or ignore the clock and just enjoy having a hassle free ride. With so many people taking part you can turn up on your own and quickly find yourself part of a group of other riders going at a similar pace.

Cycling holidays

Cycling holidays are a great way to relax, explore and meet people. You can choose from the adventurous and exotic such as cycling in countries as diverse as Nepal or Peru, ride the beaches of Costa Rica, follow the Danube, eat cheese and drink wine in France or get to know the quiet lanes of your own country. Holidays are perfect for meeting other cyclists as you will be in a small group of between eight and 20 with a dedicated cycle guide to look after the route planning and answer your questions, it is a completely stress free way to explore by bike and often friendships made on trips last long after the sun tan has faded.

Cupid Cycles

'With around 50 per cent of people coming on Skedaddle holidays' solo travellers holidays we are forever hearing about how we've become a regular cycling Cupid. It's easy to see why you'd fall in love or strike up a new friendship with someone who shares your passion for cycling, the outdoors and visiting amazing places by bike. There is an immediate common ground and there is no better way of getting to know someone than by seeing them out on their bike and checking out just what makes they tick.'
Andrew Straws – Marketing Director at cycling holiday company Saddle Skedaddle

Finding love on your bike

Forget speed dating, cycling is the perfect way to find life-long love. These cyclists have met and married the beaus they found when out on the bike, the wind in their hair and benefiting from a healthy outdoor glow. Here are their tales of romance.

Heather, 34 and **Fred Bamforth**, 46 thank bike racing for their introduction which led to wedding bells.

'I first met Fred in June 1995 at a bike race. He was winding me up about not giving him his racing licence back fast enough. I didn't see him again until the following September when I was talking to his mates, at the Monday night track league at Manchester Velodrome. There was a group of us and we just had a laugh and enjoyed the racing.

'At the track league, they would have an event for the few women riding where we would be 'motor-paced' by somebody from the top group. Fred was Divisional Scratch Race Champion so all the women always wanted to be on his wheel. One night, my friend decided that she wanted to be motor-paced by Fred, but he offered to be my partner instead, which my friend never forgave me for. Not long after that we got together, and after I graduated from university and got a job, we bought a house and in July 2004 we finally got married, nine years after we first met.

'We stopped competing around 2001 but we're now back, though we concentrate on the road rather than the track, and have even done a couple of two-up time trials together!'

Esther Keightley, 31 was working at a bike race when ex-professional rider **Fabrizio Settembrini**, 46, took her eye.

'I was at the Paris-Tours bike race doing some work for a website, and the night before the race, I was staying in the same hotel as several professional teams. At the start the following morning a masseur from the Liquigas team waved hello from his car as he was driving off. We didn't know each other, but I recognised him from other bike races.

One of his colleagues saw this and called me over. He asked if we knew each other? No. Was I single? Yes. He then gave me this masseur's number and told me to call him, as he was very shy, but a very nice man. I sent him a message and we met up for a coffee, whilst waiting for the race to finish.

Three weeks later, I went to visit Fabrizio in Bologna and we spent the next five years seeing each other every two or three weeks either in the UK or Italy. Until finally I moved to Italy in November 2011 to give birth to our daughter Clarissa on January 17, 2012. Fabrizio still works in cycling, and Clarissa and I often go to the races to see him.

Next stop the Vuelta a Espana!'

World masters track champion **Dave Le Grys**, 58, met his wife **Tracy Baker**, 48, through cycling. Here we get them to dish the dirt and find out why bike rides are better than speed dating any day.

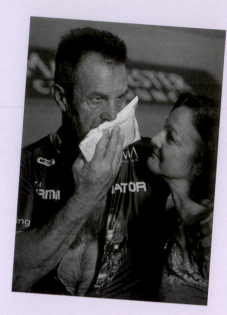

Dave on Tracy:

'I met Tracy through her daughter, Mollie, when I used to coach her. Both being cyclists, it does help because she understands the commitment needed and as Tracy rides for fun we don't clash over training or any bike issues really apart from if I buy a new pair of cycling shoes!

'Cycling is great for meeting like-minded people. It's even a perfect way to meet strangers as we all have something in common and generally speaking, we help each other out, like if you puncture or have some road side mechanical, most would stop and help out. I fancied Tracy a lot when we first met but I held back my emotions as I was coaching her daughter! I proposed to Tracy by a river in Bures in Suffolk and now we're married.

Tracy on Dave:

'When I first met Dave I thought 'Could this man smoking in my back garden and moaning that I didn't have any biscuits in my house really be a world champion and be able to train my daughter Mollie to ride on the track?' Well he did until she had to quit the sport through illness.

'I understand Dave's funny habits like leg shaving and baby-oiling his ladylike legs! I've been involved in the sport for over 20 years and it does help – though I do get jealous when he shaves his legs better than I do or blunts my razors.

We do try and go out cycling together most days – Dave rides at my pace and calls it his recovery ride (I think he's just being nice!) although he is always telling me off for riding in too big a gear. Sometimes it does get to me that I can't ride at his pace and that I'm riding with a multi time world champion but he always puts me right and says that he's just him and not to worry about it.

'I wasn't looking for anyone at the time that we met as I was going through a divorce – but Dave and I always kept in touch even when he wasn't training Mollie. He would ring and ask if I wanted to meet up but I was always at the gym or on the way to the gym. He never gave up though and we started to meet up for coffee and go to the cinema and, as they say, the rest is history.'

Chloe and **Tom Fox** decided to celebrate their honeymoon with a cycling experience. Here's 29-year-old Chloe's tale of romance and two-wheeled fun.

'Is there really anything more romantic than sleeping under the stars and life on the road in France? Living a mile alway from the ferry port in Plymouth and being keen cyclists we felt the Roscoff to Stantand would be the ultimate eco honeymoon. After a very busy year we wanted to keep it simple: the simple pleasure of two bikes, two little bags and just being together. I just loved getting to ride our bikes all day and eat what ever we wanted!

'Some days we tore up the road and 90 plus miles whistled past. Other days we meandered down riverbanks and stopped to swim and lie together in the August sun under a tree. The real delight was coming in to a city or town and being able to transform from one moment being in smelly kit to being ready for a posh dinner in my little no-iron compact dress and feeling very smug about the whole thing.

'There is a very natural rhythm to cycle touring. Nailing 40 miles before a coffee stop. Sitting in a farmer's field in the afternoon sharing a peach, deciding where to head to next is such fun. Tom decided to teach me French as we cycled and for many a mile he had me repeating after him what I wanted for dinner that evening. We planned the redevelopment of our new house and I have very fond memories of a little town we never would have discovered had we been in a car.

'The lovely bit is also taking care of each other. I had a little packet of rhubarb sweets hidden for when I needed to bribe Tom to cycle a bit further. Tom was a star at always insisting I go and have a shower while he pitched the tent and sorted out the camp. He also gave me hugs and made me plough on, even when I cried all morning from sheer tiredness.

'It's all about sharing experiences and a achievement at the same time, and what better way than by bike?'

Resources

ORGANISATIONS

British Cycling www.britishcycling.org.uk

Cycle Training UK www.cycletraining.co.uk

Cyclists' Touring Club (CTC) www.ctc.org.uk

URBAN BIKE HIRE

Boris Bikes (Barclays' Cycle Hire)

www.tfl.gov.uk/roadusers/cycling/14808.aspx

ROUTES / ROUTE-FINDING

National Cycle Network

www.sustrans.org.uk/ncn/map/national-cycle-network

Sustrans www.sustrans.org.uk

Map My Ride www.mapmyride.com

BikeHike bikehike.co.uk

Endomondo www.endomondo.com

SAFETY / INSURANCE

The Royal Society for the Prevention of Accidents www.rospa.com

Immobilise www.immobilise.com

Bikeability bikeability.dft.gov.uk/

CYCLING TO WORK

Cycle to Work Scheme www.gov.uk/government/publications/cycle-to-work-scheme-implementation-guidance

MENTAL HEALTH

The Samaritans www.samaritans.org

MIND www.mind.org.uk

Time to Change www.time-to-change.org.uk

Mind Body Dialogue www.mindbodydialogue.com

EVENTS AND HOLIDAYS

Sky Rides www.goskyride.com

Breeze www.britishcycling.org.uk/women

Cycletta humanrace.co.uk/events/cycletta

Human Race Cycling events humanrace.co.uk/events/cycling

Saddle Skedaddle www.skedaddle.co.uk

Index

Acknowledgments

Thank you to all the riders who have inspired us to write this book and who have shared their stories with us. Cycling has helped so many people find focus in life and see a path through the tough times. It has also helped many of us to shape up and find a new physique that we're proud of.

Our particular thanks goes to Lisa Thomas at Bloomsbury Publishing for believing us that cycling is the way forward in more ways than one, Steven Collins at Athlon Sport for hosting our photoshoot and our patient models Giselle Cotton, Lois Dowsett, Jack Drury, Harry Smith, Sarah Strong, Alex Dowsett, Jo Munden, Patrick Robinson, Adele Tysor Bloor, and Robert Ward.

Thank you also to Madison and Ananichoola for dressing our models and to Symon Lewis for his technical assistance.

And finally, thank you to James Golding and Jackie Stretton, two of the most courageous individuals, for showing us anything is possible.